THE CRAFT OF WRITING

THE CRAFT OF

Prentice-Hall, Inc., Englewood Cliffs, New Jersey

WRITING

WILLIAM J. BRANDT

ROBERT BELOOF

LEONARD NATHAN

CARROLL E. SELPH
University of California, Berkeley

THE CRAFT OF WRITING

William J. Brandt
Robert Beloof
Leonard Nathan
Carroll E. Selph

© 1969 by Prentice-Hall, Inc., Englewood Cliffs, N.J.

Library of Congress Catalog Card Number: 69-12624

Printed in the United States of America

Current Printing (last number):
10 9 8 7 6 5 4 3 2

PRENTICE-HALL INTERNATIONAL, INC., LONDON
PRENTICE-HALL OF AUSTRALIA, PTY. LTD., SYDNEY
PRENTICE-HALL OF CANADA, LTD., TORONTO
PRENTICE-HALL OF INDIA PRIVATE LTD., NEW DELHI
PRENTICE-HALL OF JAPAN, INC., TOKYO

to the students

INTRODUCTION

Any student intelligent enough to get into college, with a reasonably good command of English gained largely through reading, can learn to write acceptably. This does not mean that he can master, after a fashion, a genre called "student writing" that will enable him to pass a course in composition. It means that he can learn to write a kind of prose that will serve him in any situation whatsoever. Even more: he can learn to write prose that will bear an essential relationship to that of professional writers. It will not, of course, be professional in its achievement; but it will not differ from the best specimens of that art.

Nor is there any gimmickry involved in such an assurance. One begins to write prose that is professional in kind when one begins to think about one's writing as a professional writer thinks about his. The claim is that simple—and that difficult.

By the time most students come to college, they have learned that good writing is an "interesting" or "original" assemblage of good parts. No one has ever told them this in so many words, of course. But they have invested most of their time in writing classes learning what the good parts are—good choice of words, good phrasing, and good sentence structure—and they have often been graded in part upon those qualities that cannot be taught, interest and originality. The definition was implicit in their activities.

Of course, no writer thinks of his activities in this fashion. He does not put together his essay the way one would build a model airplane, out of prefabricated parts. For writing is a process, a complicated series of intellectual events taking place in time. The skill of the writer is in his control of this process.

But we must observe that the business of writing involves a division of labor among what must be called different "mental faculties." There are always at work in writing intellectual processes that are not consciously controlled. Everyone knows that neither in writing nor in speaking do we consciously put together sentences, selecting a particular noun from our store of nouns, then choosing a verb, and so forth. Sentences "come" to us fully formed. In the same way, we get "ideas," which occur to us spontaneously and cannot be arrived at by conscious, logical processes.

This inventive capacity of the human mind is responsible for what we can call the *art* of writing. Undoubtedly our previous experience, particularly our previous reading, contributes to this capacity; the more widely we have read, the greater the range of sentence patterns that are apt to be available to us. But there is little that the writer can do, directly and consciously, to cultivate this faculty and the art that depends upon it. The writer simply learns to cherish the individual gift that is given to him—with pots of coffee, peculiar hours, or whatever. It is the "given" in writing that the individual cannot transcend.

But, as every professional knows, writing is not merely—or even chiefly—art. It is impossible to write without some invention. But the essence of writing is not invention; it is *craft*. The craft of writing can be defined, briefly, as all of those activities that go into writing that can be consciously reasoned about. At the simplest level, it is craft that leads the writer to reject most of the suggestions of the inventive faculty. Unless a particular piece of writing is going very well, his conscious mind rejects at least five suggestions by the inventive faculty for every one it accepts. In its least aspect, then, the craft of writing functions as a kind of censor, selecting the useful from the mass of irrelevancies offered by the inventive faculty.

But it is not craft at this level that separates the writer from the nonwriter; few students come to college without knowing how a sentence ought to sound. The craft that distinguishes the writer is the ability to control the larger elements of his essay or story. In other words, the craft of writing is practically concerned with problems that are essentially *structural*. It lies in being able to foresee, for instance, the order required by a particular group of ideas, in knowing how to break up complex definitions into manageable units, in being able to give each element of the composition its proper weight in relationship to the other elements. It is the mark of the writer, his craft, that he can consciously resolve problems that arise from such structural considerations.

This book proposes to teach the interested student that craft of writing. It will not take him the whole way, by many a mile, but it will introduce him to the principles that must govern the kinds of writing he can be expected to encounter outside the classroom, and it will teach him to apply those principles in the kind of writing in which they are most accessible. The student who wishes to learn to write well, a matter of years and not of courses, will at least have experienced in his own writing the purposeful movement of prose—the essence of the craft of writing.

The student will observe that we have referred to the principles of writing rather than to its rules. There are, of course, what can be called "rules" in this craft as in others—rough generalizations derived from our predecessors' experience as well as our own. Such rules will be encountered from time to time in this book. But a craft is not a collection of rules. It is an ordered way of going about a task, based upon an under-standing of what is involved in it and a clear conception of its end. Craft lies in the mastery of a process directed to a specific end. Rules can be only limited helps toward this mastery.

This book, then, will teach writing as the mastery of a process; its central portion, Chapters 3 and 4, will examine that process at some length. But mastery, in turn, depends upon understanding. We must begin, then, by seeing just what is implicit in the act of writing an essay.

CONTENTS

xi

Contents

xii

Contents

xiii

THE CRAFT OF WRITING

THE CRAFT OF WRITING

1

For various reasons, most of the writing that a student does prior to coming to college is incomplete in its conception and consequently in its execution. A complete act of communication, written or not, necessarily includes three elements: the speaker or writer, the content of the communication, and an auditor or reader. But it is almost always the case that the writing a student does in high school will lack the last element, a reader. He writes examinations to display his knowledge of a particular subject; he writes essays to display his command of the fundamentals of grammar and style. The reader is not an important consideration in such writing.

It will be useful to think of partial communication of this kind, in which the reader does not seriously figure, as *declarative*. Briefly, declarative writing is writing which is not affected by a consideration of any specific audience to whom it might be directed. There might not even be an audience. "Ouch!" is ordinarily declarative. Given the forceful contact of a hammer with a thumb, "ouch," or something worse, is a common linguistic consequence even if no one else is present. In other instances there may be an audience, but it does not affect the form of the communication. "Turn left at the second stop light" would ordinarily be a declarative statement. It might be uttered in response to a question, but the form and content of such a statement would seldom be affected by a consideration of who asked it. In other words, declarative writing is a kind of self-expression in which one simply says what he thinks with a minimum of concern for who is to hear it.

A complete act of communication, on the other hand, is *persuasive*. Not only is it written for a specific audience, large or small, but the character of that audience enters importantly into the how and even the what of the writer's strategy. A letter home requesting money is a good example of persuasive writing. The student writing the letter has very vividly in mind the sort of person to whom he is writing it, and this conception powerfully affects the manner of the writing as well as what is said—or not said.

Such writing is properly called persuasive because it is undertaken to bring about some sort of consequence. The persuasive writer wants a certain group of people, his selected audience, to understand something rightly for a change or to behave differently in some respect. He wants them to understand why Socrates behaved wrongly (or rightly) in Plato's *Apology;* he wants the city council to put a stop light at a particular intersection; or he wants the draft abolished by Congress. In short, he wants to make something happen.

Of course, *declarative* and *persuasive* do not specify absolute distinctions. Any extended piece of writing will betray some awareness of an audience and hence will be persuasive to some degree. On the other hand, few people are willing to persuade at any cost to the truth as they see it; hence there is an irreducible element of declaration in their writings. But the distinction is nevertheless an important one for the writer.

There are occasions which call for declarative writing. A set of directions or a recipe can be little but declarative. Technical reports are often declarative, since the writer is usually asked to present information from which others may arrive at a decision. Furthermore, there are occasions in human life when one's back is against the wall and there is not much else to do but to declare oneself and take the consequences.

But declarative writing is nonetheless incomplete. It does not have an audience which significantly affects what is being said. But unless he keeps his audience in mind, the writer can have no very clear conception of what he must do to bring about a specific consequence. From the writer's point of view, this incompleteness of declarative writing is very serious. The reason is obvious. A carpenter can practice his craft fully only when he has some object in mind as the proposed result of that craft, be it a table or a house. The writer is in much the same situation, and declarative writing does not have in view an objective that will serve him in the actual process of writing.[1]

Persuasive writing, on the other hand, is defined by the fact that it has a definite end in view. The persuasive writer wishes to bring about a particular end. He wants a certain group of people to think in a certain way about a particular human concern or he wants them to behave in a certain way. "Intention" is the word which will henceforth be used to refer to this end. An intention is not simply the desire to make something happen; nor is it an awareness of a particular audience. An intention is the desire to bring about a particular consequence by addressing oneself to a particular audience.

Of course, the writer can never know as much as he needs to about his audience; even the writer of much experience can make serious miscalculations in his estimate of his audience.[2] But every writer must have some idea of his audience. Without such a conception, even the simplest questions are impossible to answer except by pure guesswork. For instance: Do I need

1 One must assume, of course, that there is a reason even for declarative writing. The recipe writer, for instance, may be very positively motivated by a desire to make money. But such a desire is extrinsic to the actual business of writing recipes. It cannot help him make any decision in the process of writing itself. For the student, the desire for a good grade is analogous to the recipe writer's desire for money; it may make him want to do well but cannot help him in the doing. For this reason, teachers frequently attempt to discourage the student who seems too narrowly concerned with his grade. Such a concern can be a handicap to the student because it can distract him from his proper and necessary concerns as a writer.

2 For this reason, professional writers and scholars habitually circulate their work in manuscript among friends who can approximate their larger audience. Students would do well to emulate this practice.

The Craft of Writing

to define this term? Can I allow this statement to stand unsupported, as self-evident, or do I need to argue for its truth? Do I have to explain the general situation that I wish to discuss? Such questions are obviously omnipresent in writing, and not one of them can be answered rationally except with reference to a conception of the mind or minds that the writer wishes to influence.[3]

The sense of audience in persuasive writing is not, however, merely the point of reference by which one makes local, if omnipresent, decisions. It is the thing which permits writing to be strategic rather than formulaic. A good persuasive essay will have its own structure, determined by the particular intention which led to its writing. In contrast, one recipe is much like another, since there is little to do with its elements but organize them in a simple before-and-after organization; its climax, if it has one, will be found on the table and not in the writing at all.

In short, the student who has learned to write persuasively will have learned to work out essay-structures for himself, guided in each instance by the particular intention he has in mind. Every essay he writes will be in some fashion unique. However, all of them will be responsive to principles inherent in the relationship that he will have established with the reader. It is essential that he understand these principles.

THE READER-WRITER RELATIONSHIP

It is the special mark of persuasive prose that the writer initiates the communication for his own ends, and hence he is chiefly interested in its effectiveness. The reader may be quite content with his understanding of *The Heart of Darkness* or with his attitude toward selective service; it is the writer who finds that understanding, or that attitude, deficient. It follows that the burden of the communication falls mainly upon him. The writer must be aware of that burden and govern himself accordingly.

In a negative way, the persuasive writer acknowledges this character of the reader-writer relationship by demanding as

[3] A discussion of these problems will be found in Chapter 5.

little effort of the reader as is consistent with his own intention. When a student is told to write clearly, this is what is, or ought to be, meant: don't make the reader work harder than is absolutely necessary. A complex subject demands more of the reader than a simple one; an argument about the causes of sunspots cannot be as immediately intelligible as one about the responsibility for an automobile accident. But the writer in each case is obliged by the situation to make his argument as readily understandable as possible. He will not do this out of any natural affection for his audience, whom he may privately regard in any light he chooses, but out of regard for his own interest—to convince that audience of an idea to which the writer himself is committed.

It is perhaps worth pointing out that this attitude toward communication is responsible for the writer's respect for grammar and syntax. Misused words, faulty punctuation, and so forth are not necessarily evidence of a flawed character. In most cases, they do not even prohibit communication; for example, no one would bother to complain about the punctuation in a guidebook to buried treasure. These common violations of the generally accepted rules simply make reading more difficult and force the reader to work harder than he might. Since, by definition, the reader is not usually burningly interested in the first place, a passage that must be reread is an invitation to him to abandon the attempt at communication altogether. This prospect should encourage the writer to pay attention to such details.

But adjusting to the reader takes the writer beyond considerations of clarity and easy reading. It governs the whole strategy of writing. For there are few situations, outside the classroom, in which the reader is compelled to read. Ordinarily he can put down a book or magazine at will. And since reading is a complex and difficult activity, he is usually more inclined to put down a book than to finish it. The writer must assume that this human impulse to inertia exists and, because the responsibility for communication is his, he must develop every technique at his disposal to overcome it.

One way to keep a reader reading, of course, is to be consistently interesting, paragraph by paragraph and page by page. Sometimes the uniqueness of one's experience makes this easy.

The Craft of Writing

5

Lion-hunting is very interesting to some people, and they constitute an easily satisfied audience if one's subject is a personal experience of lion-hunting. There have of course also been writers who are interesting without very much subject matter—most of them humorists. The late James Thurber's *Life in Ohio*, for instance, is a book without much point, but it is very readable because it is consistently funny. The reader attacks the tenth, or the hundredth, paragraph with enthusiasm because previous paragraphs have been interesting, and he has no reason to suppose Mr. Thurber's talent will desert him. But this is not a talent given to everyone, and it is assuredly not a talent to be taught.

Fortunately, the writer has another option. He can get and hold readers by promising them that something is about to happen and keeping his promise. Homer began *The Iliad* with precisely such a promise.

> Sing, O Goddess, of the wrath of Peleus' son Achilles, the deadly wrath that brought down upon Achaeans countless woes and sent many mighty souls of heroes down to the house of death. . . .[4]

One reads *The Iliad* in the first place to find out about the devastation caused by Achilles' wrath—to see what is going to happen. One ordinarily reads essays for the same reason. As E. M. Forster pointed out long ago in connection with the novel, the writer can always safely assume on the part of his reader a kind of brute curiosity. I may not be deeply concerned about a fictional character called Hamlet or about the United Nations or about the art of Mark Twain when I first encounter an essay on one of these subjects. But if the author can give me a strong expectation of something about to happen, he has a better chance of holding and developing my interest.

Almost all writers of prose, fiction or nonfiction, operate in this fashion; they begin their writing by setting up an expectation of something about to happen. But to propose that something is going to happen is at the same time a kind of

---

[4] *The Iliad*, trans. A. H. Chase and W. G. Perry, Jr. (New York: Bantam Books, Inc., 1960), p. 35.

guarantee. This is the reader-writer contract, the implicit agreement between them. It is a contract always implicitly operative for the reader. The writer should understand it and keep it in mind, because if he ever falters in keeping his end of the bargain he is very apt to lose his audience forever.

THE READER-WRITER CONTRACT

One can look at the way curiosity functions for the writer in this fashion. In setting up the introduction of an essay, he proposes a problem about which the reader will be vaguely curious. "Why was Plato driven to use rhetoric to attack rhetoric?" "What prevents the United Nations from dealing with certain kinds of conflicts?" Or whatever problem he chooses. By his introduction the writer implicitly assures the reader that what follows will resolve the problem in some way, without taking more time about it than necessary. The reader, by beginning to read, agrees to the contract thus offered. And that contract will be in force as long as the reader remains curious about the resolution of the problem, which means, in practice, as long as what is written seems to be actively directed toward that resolution.

To put it another way, a writer can be reasonably sure his readers are with him as long as what he writes moves, or at least seems to move, toward a conclusion. To maintain a sense of movement, of progression, is the essence of the writer's art.

But what do we mean when we say that prose moves? The expression is most readily understood in terms of simple narrative writing. A narrative moves, in the first place, because it deals with events in time, with before and after. "This happened and this happened and this happened," the writer tells us, and we read further to see what is going to happen next. But the simple temporal sequence is by no means the whole of the narrative art. It is also necessary that these happenings in time be related. We cannot be interested for long in things happening unless we can see causal relationships among those things. A simple narrative lays before us what might be called a chain of events or happenings—a chain because they are linked together in one fashion or another.

But there is a further requirement upon the narrative writer,

The Craft of Writing

or at least the writer of traditional narrative. That requirement is that this causal chain the reader is following be directed someplace, that the actions which are being followed terminate in some sort of resolution.

Movement in non-narrative prose (in essays, for all practical purposes) is more difficult to describe, but it is similar to the movement of narrative. It arises from a sense of relatedness among parts, and it presupposes a resolution. An essay moves when one paragraph leads to the next, and to the one after that, with the whole governed by the writer-reader contract. A student essay will provide a useful example, both of movement and of its sudden demise:

> Even an inexperienced reader of poetry shortly finds that he likes one poem more than another, and furthermore, that the matter of liking or not liking is not necessarily connected with the relative excellence of the poems. He may recognize that what others say about Milton's "Lycidas," for example, is true, that it is a great poem. But it is not a great poem for him. He may prefer a poem like Sir Walter Raleigh's "The Lie" even while he recognizes that it is not as good as "Lycidas." What is it that causes a person to enjoy one poem and not another?
>
> First it is necessary to deal with the nature of poetry. Most poetry is basically praise. The poet praises a certain quality or a person possessing a quality. For example, Dylan Thomas's "Do Not Go Gentle into that Good Night" praises a passionate commitment to life. Sometimes a poet praises a certain attitude indirectly by assuming it himself, as does Frost in "Two Tramps in Mud-Time." In any case, most poetry is asking for the reader's approval of something.
>
> To appreciate a poem the reader must be able to accept, or identify with, the quality being praised. If he cannot do this, he will be unable to enjoy the poem. It is relatively easy for one to accept Thomas' poem to his father, for instance, because most people can appreciate being committed to something. However, Yeats's "A Prayer for My Daughter" is probably not very popular in America because not many people can appreciate an aristocratic life.
>
> But if the appreciation of poetry depended simply upon liking that which praised qualities we already appreciated, everyone would like a very limited number of

poems. But this isn't the case. Many people like poems which praise things which are almost antithetical. The same person may like both the Thomas poem, which praises commitment, and poems which praise resignation. The reader does not merely enjoy poems which praise qualities (or attitudes) he already has, but those that he can *imagine* having. Imagination is the capacity which is required for the enjoyment of poetry.

Of course, psychologists do not like to talk about imagination. They prefer to think of the mind as something which records facts. To admit that it is capable of other kinds of activities seems to them to break it up into different things. The most important reason that they do not like words like "imagination," however. . . .

This is not a particularly good paper, but it illustrates both the nature of the reader-writer contract and its failure.

In the first paragraph, the student sets up his problem (perhaps even too explicitly in the last sentence); this is his contract. The paper proceeds to make good that contract through the next three paragraphs. The first of these paragraphs defines his subject, poetry, from a point of view adequate to the paper; the second relates the reader to this definition; the third raises a revelant fact. Most readers would follow this progression of ideas easily; the paper to this point moves adequately enough.

But most readers, too, would sense a radical discontinuity between the fourth paragraph and the last one quoted. Psychologists can have nothing to do with the contract proposed in the first paragraph, and hence the paper is at this point dead. One does not have to analyze paragraph relationships to perceive this; a reader of even moderate sophistication will detect a failure of orderly progression toward a pre-established end, a failure of movement. Even if he is the instructor, he is justified in abandoning the paper at this point because the writer has violated the contract that he himself proposed.

There are other kinds of movement, or perhaps illusions of movement, available to the writer. He can move by association —from spring to cherry blossoms to Japan, for instance, because both spring and Japan are connected to cherry blossoms in our minds. Very skilled writers appear at times to be circling their subject, moving closer and closer to it as they move

The Craft of Writing

from one way of looking at it to another. Perhaps most of what we read today, in publications such as *Life* and *The Atlantic*, does not move at all, but keeps readers by a skillful illusion of movement. Movement or the illusion of it—there must be one or the other. The ability to keep prose moving purposefully is not the whole of the art of writing, but it is the essence of it, and there is no art without it.

Conclusion

There is little point in asking students to learn in a quarter or a semester the complicated skills the professional writer brings to bear in an associationist novel or a skilled piece of reportorial writing with its pseudoconnections and pseudomovement (although the last chapter will consider these skills briefly). But neither is there any point in teaching him something called "student writing," which has nothing to do with the activities of the professional writer. A student should learn the art of writing, as it is practiced by professional writers, in its simpler forms. Hence a writing course, and not a course in grammar or logic, ought to teach the student how to make prose move by establishing the most direct and easily managed connections.

But even here there is a difficulty. Experienced writers establish this connectedness and maintain this movement by a kind of intuition developed by years of reading and writing. An experienced writer *feels* his prose moving along well, or he feels it losing momentum. These feelings he has learned to respect utterly. When he feels his prose lose movement, he does not slog on. He backs up and changes his attack. He will probably go away and come back when he has a fresh point of view. He has gotten off the line of thought that will lead him to his conclusion; this is what a loss of movement means. He knows there is no point in persisting with what has become a dead end.

An inexperienced writer has no such intuition. It is likely that he has never written a piece of prose which genuinely moved. Nor does his teacher have any means to give him a kind of intuition which he has picked up by years of experience. A writer learns to make prose move by making it move, and for most so-called "kinds of writing" the principles of movement are not readily teachable.

The one kind of writing in which movement in prose can be taught directly, in our experience, is argumentation. Just what argumentation is will be considered in some detail in the next chapter. Here it is sufficient to point out its merit as a way of learning to write. If the student will work out a statement of what he wants to say, his intention, that is very precise, that statement will define for him the elements of an argumentative essay. Because what the paper must do is thereby defined for him, he can concentrate on finding an ordering of those elements that will permit his paper to really move. Hence the rest of this book, with the exception of the last chapter, will be concerned with argumentative writing. Hopefully, the student will learn from it not merely how to write an argument, but how to make prose—any kind of prose —move.

2 | ARGUMENTATION

The whole craft of writing depends, then, upon its purposiveness, upon the fact that the writer has committed himself to bringing something about, if he can, by persuading his audience of the credibility of a certain statement. In writing, the end must come before the beginning, at least in the writer's mind. The writer must have two things; he must have an audience, and he must have a statement relevant in some way to that audience.

It will be useful to consider for a moment this statement, which is such an important part of the writer's intention. (It will be called hereafter his *thesis* or *thesis statement*.) It can be briefly described as a subject-verb-object sentence which is both problematic enough and important enough—to the audience—to justify the time it will take to read it in the form which the writer chooses.

The important qualifications will be considered in a later chapter; it is enough for the purposes of this one to note that a thesis is after all merely a sentence. "John loves Mary" could be a thesis if it met the qualifications, as it does not (except for John and Mary, of course). And a sentence merely proposes that a specific relationship exists between two terms. If I were to attempt to persuade an audience of the truth of my "John statement," for instance, my job would be to show that a specific sort of relationship does in fact exist between two specific sorts of objects.

But our culture gives us several ways to establish this relationship, and at least theoretically the writer who has decided upon his thesis and selected his audience (the two comprising his intention) still has to select the genre in which he can accomplish his intention most effectively.

MEANS OF PERSUASION   A concrete illustration will show how persuasion works in different genres. Let us suppose that we have a problem of somewhat more general interest than the John-Mary relationship; let us suppose that we have decided, through our writings, to work for world peace. We make it our intention to persuade a large group of people to sacrifice every other consideration to securing a general peace.

One perhaps unpromising way to do this would be to write a novel or a short story about war. In my novel or short story I might never even mention the desirability of peace; rather, I would attempt to present the horrors of war as experienced by particular people and allow the reader to generalize from those horrors. My object would be to lead the reader to some kind of reliving of the experiences about which I wish him to think in a certain way.

It is unlikely that I would proceed in this particular way, it should be pointed out, because the highest levels of fiction and poetry ordinarily do not function well as a call to action. (*On the Beach* and *Uncle Tom's Cabin* provide examples of the level of literature usually effective in causes.) Fiction and poetry are ordinarily concerned on the first level with understanding rather than action. But understanding properly precedes action, and creative writing is hence powerfully persuasive in the long run. Most educated people, if they thought about it, would find certain literary experiences to have been profoundly important in shaping their beliefs and lives.

But there are alternative methods of persuasion. Reporting or exposition dominates most of the better journals in the twentieth century. If I were a reportorial writer concerned about world peace, I might do an article about a particularly promising peace organization. I would describe the organization, speak of its growth, talk about its influence, if any, and perhaps make a brief statistical prediction about the consequences of the next war. (It will be noted that no matter how well I know my thesis in reportorial writing, I still have a wide range of choice in the materials I will use.)

I would probably do my reporting as though I were the most objective person in the world; such is the current fashion. But my writing would still be persuasive, directed toward a particular end, even though I openly declared that end, that thesis, at no point in my essay. It would be persuasive because what the reporter (as that term is used here) says is, "Let's look at it this way." There are always several possible ways to look at any situation worth our attention in the first place, and the way one looks has a good deal to do with the attitude one finally adopts. Furthermore, every writer must select, and that selection necessarily arises from a judgment about the subject he writes about.

It will be observed that reporting is somewhat more abstract, more removed from the concrete situation, than is fiction. The reporter makes no attempt to recreate reality in the reader's imagination. Reportorial writing is habitually descriptive, written from the outside, but it is still concerned with presenting the thing, or the situation, itself.

The third obvious means of persuasion is argumentation. An argument differs from the other genres in that it presents the writer's thesis explicitly. It is unlikely that a reportorial writer, much less a novelist, would even declare his thesis. The writer of argumentation not only proclaims it (or a paraphrase of it) explicitly; he makes it the basis for his organization. He attempts to persuade to his point of view by arguing for his thesis directly.

This characteristic can be clarified by an example. As was pointed out earlier, a thesis is a subject-verb-object sentence,

Argumentation

and that sentence thereby asserts that there is a particular relationship, represented by the verb, which exists, or ought to exist, between two objects, usually the nouns. These parts of speech become the parts of an argument. If the thesis were "A world peace organization is necessary to avoid atomic destruction," these terms would be reflected in particular parts of the essay. There would be a section which would define "a world peace organization," one which defined "atomic destruction," and one which attempted to relate these terms in the way proposed by the verb. In other words, it is the mark of argumentation that the important elements of the thesis—nouns, verbs, certain kinds of qualifiers and certain conjunctions—become the elements of the essay. The way in which these elements are ordered, of course, is a different matter.

AN ARGUMENTATIVE THESIS But a difficulty should be apparent to the thoughtful student. How in the world is one going to define meaningfully in the context "a world peace organization"? Or "atomic destruction"? The thesis turns out to be too vague to mean much when one thinks of it as defining a writing job. One might attempt to write something other than argumentation from such a vague conception; an argumentative thesis has to be more precise.

A distinction will be of some use: what we have been considering is not really a thesis at all; it is an opinion. The distinction is that an opinion is too vague to write an argument from. All of us operate in terms of opinions, of vague attitudes toward this or that. And they serve us well for the most part. But when an opinion is challenged, we very shortly discover its inadequacy.

Nevertheless theses are related to opinions; in some sense they are the unformulated, almost unconscious bases for opinions. This becomes apparent in any serious discussion. If I should proclaim the above opinion among friends who really cared about it, I would find myself immediately challenged. "What do you mean, 'a world peace organization'? We've got one: the United Nations, and it doesn't seem to be doing much good." Being thus challenged, I would find myself forced to reformulate. But it would not be a process of inventing a new statement; it would be a process of discovering precisely what lay behind the statement first made. I would be forced to discover the thesis that lay behind the opinion all the time, whether I was aware of it or not.

In the next chapter we will consider the process by which one discovers his thesis. Let us assume that we have completed the process and arrived at our point of discovery. We will recognize that point because we are satisfied with the formulation; if someone should ask for further clarification, we could only say the same thing over again.

"In the long run, an organization with the legal system to adjudicate minor disputes and the power to enforce its decisions can prevent major conflicts." That is the thesis that we had in mind all along. It differs in two ways from the mere opinion with which we began. First, it is qualified, if only by the phrase "in the long run." Our opinions habitually claim more than we would really like to insist upon. Second, our terms are more precise. The first term has become more precise because it limits the vague term "world peace organization" to a much more specific kind of organization. The object of the verb is more expressive of our original intention. "Atomic destruction" is perhaps implicit in "major conflicts," but it is not the same thing. Our organization is immediately aimed at preventing conflicts, not atomic destruction.

In summary: the thesis of an argument represents the specific intention of the writer, and in turn it defines the elements of the essay. But it must be precise. A reportorial writer can perhaps begin with an opinion; an argumentative writer needs a thesis.

FROM THE THESIS TO THE THESIS STATEMENT One further characteristic of argumentation must be noted. An argument does not merely declare itself explicitly; it gives reasons. Like most kinds of communication, it gives reasons as it goes along, from paragraph to paragraph. But argumentation also advances a principal reason which functions as a part of its total statement. We have formulated a thesis: "In the long run, only an organization with the legal system to adjudicate minor disputes and the power to enforce its decisions can prevent major conflicts." This is a thesis; it is the conclusion one hopes that his readers will assent to after they have read the essay. It becomes a thesis *statement* when we add to it our principal reason for believing it to be true—a because clause. We can make our thesis into a thesis statement, for instance, by adding the clause, "because only such an organization can sufficiently diminish the effect of national pride which escalates minor conflicts."

Such a reason, a *because* clause, is a part of the total thesis statement because the new terms it contains will also have to be defined and related to other terms, and hence they represent elements of the structure of the argument. If we were to analyze the structure of a paper written from this thesis statement, we would be able to find a paragraph or paragraphs defining the "national pride which escalates minor conflicts" as well as the paragraph or paragraphs defining "an organization with the legal system." In other words, the *because* clause of a thesis statement is an integral part of the writer's intention even though it merely supports his major point.

LOGIC IN ARGUMENTATION   The reason in the thesis statement is ordinarily a *because* clause, but not every *because* clause is an adequate reason. Only the briefest excursion into logic is necessary to clarify the distinction.

The basic deductive figure in classical logic is the *syllogism*, and its classic example runs as follows:

> Major premise: All men are mortal.
> Minor premise: The Greeks are men.
> Conclusion: The Greeks are mortal.

One observes that the syllogism is composed of three statements, and these three statements include three, and only three, terms. If these statements bear a proper relationship to each other, and if the premises are true, then the conclusion will also be true. In other words, the truth of the conclusion is deduced from (because it is somehow implicit in) the premises.

We can readily make a syllogism into an *enthymeme* by simply omitting our major premise:

| Minor premise: | All Greeks are men. |
| Conclusion: | All Greeks are mortal. |

An *enthymeme* is simply an abbreviated form of the syllogism; one of the premises, usually the major premise in argumentation, is omitted.[1] Nothing is really lost by the abbreviation. We still have three terms, and if we appropriately combine the two terms that occur only once, *men* and *mortal*, we can readily reconstruct the missing major premise.

But this enthymeme can be expressed in another way without altering the logical relationships of the syllogism. We can say, "All Greeks are mortal *because* they are men." In this form, of course, it is a thesis statement. To state the matter from the writer's point of view, a good thesis statement is necessarily a kind of enthymeme.

Of course, a thesis statement will never be an enthymeme of which a logician could approve. It utilizes the logical relationships of the enthymeme, but these relationships are much looser in argumentation than in logic, because argumentation is concerned with probability, not proof. Furthermore, the logician could not tolerate the kinds of qualification which the honest writer is habitually forced to make.

But what, exactly, does this disguised and abbreviated syllogism do for the writer of argumentation? To find the answer, let us look again at the full syllogism, this time concerning ourselves not with Greeks but with peculiar beings from outer space, the Ums. No one knows precisely what these Ums are, or where they came from, but a large number of people seem to regard them as angels.

As has been said already, the writer begins by knowing what he wants to say about the problem that interests him, the attitude toward it that he wants his audience to share. So we begin by drawing a forthright conclusion in the matter: "Ums are not angels." But why not? We need some sort of reason to support this conclusion—a minor premise, in fact. So we decide that "Ums are not angels because they are not immortal." How does such a reason really support the conclusion? By

---

[1] In logic, an enthymeme is a syllogism with any one of the three statements omitted. Hence, it can be a major premise and a minor premise, with no conclusion expressed.

relating the doubtful matter, the nature of Ums, to a major premise which is self-evident: angels are, by definition, immortal.

We need to be careful when we make statements about logic; logicians are scrupulous in their definitions. But from the point of view of the argumentative writer, the significance of the syllogism (and the enthymeme as well) is that it permits us to establish a doubtful proposition by relating it to a certain one.

THE THESIS STATEMENT
AND
THE WRITER'S AUDIENCE

The argumentative writer does not, of course, deal with certainties, in his conclusion or his premises. His *because* clause cannot relate his conclusion to an immutable truth. Rather, it relates his conclusion to a proposition which his audience as a whole will accept as probably true. This is the mark of an adequate *because* clause: the major premise to which it implicitly appeals will strike an audience as a reasonable proposition, without further support. The writer seldom bothers to spell out his major premise precisely, because his audience will take it for granted.

Obviously, the careful writer will deduce his major premise for himself before he builds a whole argument on it. For the thesis previously proposed he would observe that his three terms were "an organization with the legal system," "major conflicts," and "national pride which escalates minor conflicts," and he would further observe that the first term occurred both in his conclusion and his *because* clause. His major premise, consequently, would relate the other two terms. It would be something like this: "Major conflicts ordinarily result from the escalation of minor conflicts." If his audience accepts this, he is in business.

When a writer is really concerned to persuade his audience, his *because* clause seldom errs through simple unacceptability. It is much more apt to fail because it does not really give a reason. Often it merely restates the conclusion in different words. In effect, it asserts that Ums are not angels because they are not angelic; *angels* and *angelic* are not substantively different terms, and hence the writer really has only his original terms. No major premise, with which the audience might agree, is implied. Sometimes the *because* clause simply lacks any real connection to the conclusion when it is closely regarded.

For the writer of argumentation, the *because* clause is apt to be the most difficult element of the whole thesis statement. If the thesis is a good one, it is apt to seem to the writer his ultimate statement upon the subject. To find a *because* clause for that thesis, he must go beyond the ultimate statement. But the step must be taken; he must find the reason that will link him to his audience and make it possible for them to accept the thesis itself. The *because* clause is not an irrational requirement the instructor has invented to make writing difficult; it is an essential connection which makes communication persuasive.

Conclusion

Let us recapitulate. The essence of writing is movement, and movement depends upon not merely a pre-established end, a conclusion of interest to the audience; it requires a steady progression toward that end. No reader will stay very long with a piece of writing which doesn't seem to have any point or seems to be taking an excessive amount of time getting to that point. A writing course must concern itself with this primary obligation laid upon the writer by the contract that he makes with the reader.

It is the peculiar advantage of argumentation that it allows the writer to determine the elements of his structure from the end that he proposes for himself—*if that end is defined with sufficient precision,* if it is a thesis and not merely an opinion. His *because* clause, furthermore, with which he completes his thesis statement, make it possible for him to begin from a point of agreement with his audience and lead that audience toward a conclusion which, presumably, it did not initially concede.

The thesis statement functions for the writer in two ways. The first way is negative. He knows that every section or every paragraph of the paper should be related to a specific element of the thesis statement. He also knows that an "idea" which occurs to him in the course of his writing, and which is not so related, is irrelevant. He is therefore not at sea, selecting arbitrarily from a great number of possible "things to say." His thesis statement has already, in some sense, defined his essay for him.

Second, the thesis statement, in its definition of the elements of his paper, proposes a series of writing jobs which are already logically or at least grammatically related to each other. The writer's problem is not to invent some sort of order, it is to translate these logical and grammatical relationships into linear ones, into a before and after. The thesis statement does not indicate this order of presentation, of course—the ordering is the major creative act in the craft of writing—but it determines the elements out of which this order is to be constructed. And the writer can be sure that his linear order is, in some sense, there, already implicit in the thesis statement itself.

The realization of a linear order, of a before and after which is not arbitrary, is at the same time the realization of a kind of forward momentum, of an apparently inevitable progression from element to element toward a conclusion. If the writer is really working out a linear order from a thesis statement, he experiences this momentum. Before one paragraph is half-written, he knows the paragraph which *must* come next. In the beginning of the writing course, the student is frequently puzzled when the instructor speaks of a paper which moves. This confusion disappears when he has written even one paper with a real linear order. At that point he has experienced the thrust of ideas almost organizing themselves (it seems) toward a conclusion. The profession of writing may begin in this experience.

3 | GETTING A THESIS

From what has been said in the previous chapter, the student may have gathered not only that getting a thesis statement is essential to argumentative writing but also that it may be a difficult task. It may be taxing, but not in an onerous or unrewarding sense. Formulating a thesis statement is a creative act, often an act of self-discovery. There can be no set of rules governing such a process and guaranteeing the outcome, but the student need not be utterly abandoned at this critical point in the writing process. We cannot propose a set of prescriptive rules which will do the job for him, but we can follow the intellectual process which may result in a thesis statement in a particular instance. When the student sets out on his own act of discovery, he will at least have been through a comparable process.

THE WRITING SITUATION   Students are frequently puzzled by the fact that so much time is taken up in a writing class talking about other things. Plato's *Meno* is not presented as an example to be emulated on the first paper. Instead, the class spends a lot of time getting at what, precisely, Plato is up to in that dialogue and whether or not it agrees with him. What do Plato's opinions, or any writer's opinions we might choose to study, have to do with learning to write?

Everything. Before anything good can come out of a writing class, the students must at least sense the presuppositions of the writer in this civilization. And the first presupposition is this: we do not really *know*, surely and indubitably, the answer to any important question. Other cultures know such answers, or think that they do, and writing is consequently a very different enterprise for them. But we, collectively, do not.

What we have, instead of the single answer to each question that many of us would like, is an extended dialogue about major questions, in the course of which a good many answers are proposed. Of course, many of the greatest men in Western civilization have been uncomfortable with this situation. The Plato of the *Republic*, for instance, would have greatly simplified Greek life, in the interest of order, by having "correct" opinions taught and "incorrect" ones suppressed. But Plato's political theory was countered by another formulated by Aristotle, and Plato himself became simply another voice in the great dialogue. Some two thousand years later, Sigmund Freud proposed "the answer" to human conduct. But within a few years his disciples, Jung and Adler, proposed quite different interpretations, and the three of them were in turn absorbed into the dialogue.

It is probable that large numbers of human beings will continue to dislike this situation. The problem is that we must act, and our acts must be based upon answers, conscious or not, to the questions considered in the great human dialogue. We must either be religious or irreligious; we must try to understand others and ourselves; we must decide what is good, however we disguise our judgment by altering terms; we must vote for the good life by trying to live it. It would be very comfortable to be able to act upon the basis of immutable truth, but it is not available to us.

It is the presupposition of humanistic studies that the great dialogue with its multiplicity of answers is a precious thing.

Getting a Thesis

If there are a half-dozen major answers to the question, "What is the good life?" then I as a reader have a choice. Indeed, the choice is forced upon me; I must formulate my own answer to the question out of the multiplicity of answers offered, on the basis of my own experience. Where there is no answer, I can formulate my own. To the extent that I can do that, I am my own man; I am free.[1]

The student who would learn to write is really preparing himself to enter into this great dialogue. He must enter it, at first, passively, as a reader. He must learn to read Dostoevsky, for instance, not as an ultimate authority on a subject, but as an important voice on important questions. He must first be sure that he understands Dostoevsky, but he must go further; he must decide whether or not what Dostoevsky says is true and useful *in terms of his own experience.*

This is not a matter of standing outside a work and judging it, but of trying it on, of testing it against one's own views. The reader should not emerge unaffected by the reading of any great work. But neither should he emerge a carbon copy of the writer he has been reading. The ultimate aim of reading a book is self-discovery—and perhaps self-creation as well. One discovers oneself, and grows in the process, by becoming seriously involved in a kind of dialogue with writers of far greater capacities than anyone he is likely to know firsthand.

The importance, in a writing class, of a genuine response to what is read cannot be overestimated. To put the matter as forthrightly as possible: the student who can become engrossed by at least some of the perennial issues raised by the great dialogue, who learns to care about them, can be taught to write. The student who cannot become really concerned about anything beyond his own immediate well-being will never learn to write anything more than school exercises. As has been said, it is the peculiar mark of the writer that he cares; he wants to have an effect upon someone else. The art of writing is principally the art of persuasion, which begins in commitment to the questions.

---

[1] Of course, all of us limit our freedom by refusing to consider certain opinions as provisional; we close our ears to elements of the debate. The student should never attempt to write about such opinions.

Getting a Thesis

THE INITIAL RESPONSE   The student's first obligation, then, is to close with the work assigned; this will be the point of departure for his own active participation in the dialogue. This means that he must understand the author's point—his thesis, if you will. Essays do not present much of a problem in this matter; the writer's point is usually clear enough, although the force of his argument may be missed. But fiction requires more sophistication from the reader. A large part of the trick is to avoid side issues. In Sophocles' *Antigone*, for instance, the heroine believes that she is ordered by the gods to bury her brother. The student who doubts that the gods really care about such things must learn not to be unduly troubled by his disagreement with the author, because that is not what Sophocles is concerned about. He is concerned about the relationship of an individual to his moral codes, of which brother-burying is merely an instance. To read a work well is to learn to separate the essential from the non-essential, *from the author's point of view*. We must make that separation even to begin to understand what is being said.

But when I have read a work and have understood it, then I am obliged to make some sort of response to it. And this first response is a very important one. It will certainly be inadequate as a basis for writing, but it will not be irrelevant to writing. The proposition that the writer finally chooses to argue for—his thesis—may bear scarcely any resemblance to the proposition which was his initial response to the subject. But there is almost always a relationship. The thesis statement is the end of a long process of discovery and refinement which begins with the writer's initial response to a problem. Hence, the common experience of students in writing classes is that they *discover* what they want to say. It is something that was there all the time, behind the crudities of the writer's initial response, even though he was unaware of it at the time.

THE DEVELOPMENT   The process of discovery is best
OF THE THESIS   understood in concrete terms. Let
us say that the reading assignment has been Henry David Thoreau's "On the Duty of Civil Dis-

Getting a Thesis

obedience." As a conscientious student, I will have read the essay before class discussion. I will have considered its thesis, have been troubled by it surely, but finally I will find that I do not agree with what Mr. Thoreau proposes. But I will probably be vague about why I disagree. My first opinion may be no more specific than the question, "What would happen if everyone behaved like that?" And I will go to class, virtuously secure in my opinion.

But I will undoubtedly encounter other opinions in the first class discussion. (If the class itself does not provide sufficient variety, the instructor is obliged to.) So, in effect, the characters in the great dialogue will change, temporarily, from writer-reader to reader-reader. I will be invited not merely to take a position but to defend it on the spot from other opinions. The student who declines this opportunity from timidity or lethargy is foolish indeed.

So I declare myself. I point out that Thoreau's advice is bad because everyone cannot follow it without destroying society. To withdraw allegiance every time we think the government is behaving immorally would make a shambles out of society; people would be withdrawing allegiance over almost everything. There are people who think public education is immoral. And so forth.

But another student will probably point out the difficulty with my initial position. Thoreau himself made a point which would have to be considered: if every man simply obeys the government, then every man exists for the government. The government becomes more important than its parts. That should not be permitted to happen. And another student might bring up the Nuremburg trials. Surely I don't think any action whatsoever can be justified because the government orders it. Weren't the people who ran the concentration camps in World War II guilty of a crime, even though their government ordered them to do it?

These are solid objections, and I will probably be tempted to abandon my position altogether and agree with Thoreau. There is no law, of course, against changing one's mind when reasons are given. But these objections do not refute my original position; they are merely objections to it. So I shall be a little stubborn. I may feel somewhat at a loss in the class

Getting a Thesis

discussion for a fitting response to these objections, but I will not surrender my position.

But I will also modify it. Perhaps I will observe that I have been led into an extreme position because Thoreau's position is at the other extreme. I still do not believe that an individual is obliged to resist any action of the government which he finds morally objectionable to the limit of civil disobedience. But neither do I believe that one is obliged, willy-nilly, to do whatever one's particular government orders. I have made a useful discovery about my own convictions.

Sooner or later the instructor will abandon Thoreau's essay; the function of discussion in a writing class is emphatically not to resolve questions. And I do not as yet have a thesis. I have a refined opinion, which, if I thought it worth working out, might be, "Thoreau's conception of the obligation of civil disobedience is an excessively simple one." My problem is now to develop that insight, learned partly in class, into something sufficiently precise to be worth writing a paper about. And I must do it on my own.

There are two habits which can be of immense value to me in this endeavor. In the first place, I need to get into the habit of jotting things down. I should jot down, in the briefest possible fashion, every idea that occurs to me, every example, every objection. I should write out the definitions I work out. This habit of writing things down will force me to think creatively, and the notes can help the instructor help me if it should come to that.

The second indispensable habit is the budgeting of time. The whole process of writing even a brief paper can take fifteen hours. If I am so foolish as to put off until Sunday a paper due Monday I will in the first place make very bad use of my time—the writing will take longer than it otherwise might—and I will be very apt to panic when thought does not advance as rapidly as I had counted on. The time given to a writing class should be spread out. A couple of hours immediately after class discussion can be very useful; the problem will still be an immediate one. But I should plan to accomplish the whole task over at least three days. It is a peculiar and useful characteristic of the human brain that you can deposit a problem in it, go away from that problem for some time by think-

Getting a Thesis

ing about other things, and come back to find that the brain, in its own mysterious way, has at least made some progress toward its solution.

The search for a thesis is just that—a search. It exists, but the writer has no map to guide him to it. At least some of the ways of searching can be specified. When the writer comes to a dead end in his thinking, he can quite deliberately do one of four things. (1) He can examine his position, his dilemma as it has become, and see if it is a particular kind of problem, if he can determine in advance the kind of solution he is looking for. As will be seen, whenever he is trying to work out some ground between two extremes, he can know in advance that what he needs is a criterion by which to make a distinction. (2) He can force himself to define troublesome terms. A writer thinking about a problem frequently finds himself in a circle, where one opinion leads to another, which unfortunately leads him back to the first, or even to its antithesis. In such cases, the problem is usually a shifty term. In any case, it is always useful for him to work out careful definitions of the big words he is using. (3) He can try to find examples. He should always be testing his generalizations against experience. Frequently a concrete instance will provide the insight he needs to discover his thesis. "Do I know anyone who is like that, or who has done that sort of thing?" (4) He can ask himself "why" and insist on an answer. "But why do I object to Nazis who killed helpless men, women, and children because Hitler ordered it?" To ask "why" of himself is the most difficult strategy the writer, or thinker, has available, but an honest answer will lead to an important advance in his understanding of his own convictions.

The writer simply working out his own position can use these questions to clarify it. But the writer responding to someone else should use these questions both ways—to examine his own position and the one he responds to. A careful definition of Thoreau's terms, for instance, is as important as a careful definition of one's own.

DEVELOPING A THESIS   It will we useful to indicate how these strategies can be used by working out the thesis about the essay "On the Duty of Civil

Getting a Thesis

28

Disobedience." But the student should remember that the process of discovery is a much more complicated one than can be represented here. The point of what follows is to show how one approaches the problem, not to describe accurately an invariable sequence.

To summarize: I know, in the first place, that I think Thoreau's position is both too extreme and too simple. But in the course of refuting him, I have proposed a position which is also too simple. The first question, about the *kind* of problem faced, is a useful one here. One of the things I will probably want at some point is a criterion or principle which will prevent me from murdering children at the government's behest but will not require me to renounce my allegiance because it fights a Mexican War I do not approve of. But a good deal of thought convinces me that I have not, as yet, a clue as to what it might be.

So I will abandon that line of inquiry for the moment and go back to my opinion of the simplicity of Thoreau's position. What is so simple about it? This is to ask for a definition—his definition, to begin with—and I must return to the text. But if I have read it carefully to begin with, I need not read it so closely again. I will thumb through it, reading parts relevant to the definition I am after. When I first read the book, I was trying to understand Thoreau's position. Now I will try to make him answer *my* questions.

And if I study the book long enough, I will make a discovery. I will realize that Thoreau makes an absolute split between government and society. This split is reflected in his insistence upon the uselessness of government at the beginning of the essay, in his willingness in many other places to stay in society after he has withdrawn allegiance from the government. (I should note the page numbers for future reference.) So Thoreau proposes to renounce his allegiance to the *Commonwealth* of Massachusetts but he does not propose to renounce his relationship to the *society* of Massachusetts. This is an important distinction and should be incorporated into my rough definition: "Thoreau's civil disobedience is a refusal to support in any way a government which does not behave morally, as he judges, in a matter of importance, without thereby renouncing the social relationships and services within that government."

Getting a Thesis

29

That definition should open up a good many lines of inquiry. In the first place it should lead me to work out my own definition of civil disobedience, in contradistinction to that of Thoreau. I do not believe in Thoreau's distinction between government and society. Government and society create each other, and the individual cannot legitimately renounce one without renouncing the other. My own definition must reflect this emphasis: "Civil disobedience is total withdrawal from society as well as government when moral outrage will no longer permit one to support, even passively, the activities of one or the other."

But having come this far, I will perhaps see that there are now two courses open to me, two papers which I can write (unless the instructor has specified very closely the subject he is interested in). I can write a paper about Thoreau's opinion. I have, at least in a general way, the point which will permit me to criticize Thoreau effectively, and such a paper should be relatively easy to write. (In general, a negative position is easier to argue than a positive one.) But a refutation of Thoreau would not tell me where I stand, and I would like to know. Therefore, I elect the more difficult option (hoping the instructor recognizes that I am doing so) and set off on the search for a position on civil disobedience which is my own.

But I resume my search with a new insight: government and society cannot, in my opinion, be separated. But so what? What difference does this insight make to my position besides making civil disobedience much more difficult for me than it was for Thoreau? One can wrestle with a question like this for a long time and not get anywhere. Better not to wrestle too long. Better to change the question somewhat. What did the government-society distinction do for Thoreau's position? Back to the text. A little thinking will answer this question for me. Because Thoreau regards government and society as utterly distinct, he is able to argue that the government is, literally, no good. Society is clearly good for man, even for Thoreau, but government he can take or leave. But since I hold another opinion about the relationship of government to society, I necessarily hold another opinion about the value of government. Government is, for me, an agency of good.

By and large, of course. Not everything any government

does will strike me as good, but most of the governments that I know about I would assume do more good than bad, since societies depend upon them. Hitler's government was not an agency of good, of course—and if I am not too sleepy at this point, I will observe that I have discovered the distinction I looked for in vain when I first considered the problem of civil disobedience. I can propose the point at which a rational and moral man ought to refuse allegiance to a government. At the same time, I have discovered my thesis. "Civil disobedience, with its attendant withdrawal from society itself, is justified only when that government and its society is the instrument of more bad than good." Not quite that: ". . . only when that government and its society cannot be expected to bring about more good than bad." That's better; one should act in terms of the future, not merely the present. I have my thesis.

FROM THESIS
TO THESIS STATEMENT

I might well go to bed at this point, but I should remember on my way that I am not finished with my labors. I must still accomplish that crucial move from the thesis, declaring my conviction, to the thesis statement, which includes my reason for believing the thesis to be true. Since the thesis usually presents itself to the writer as his primal insight into the nature of things, going beyond it is never easy.

A word of caution is necessary at this point. Even the most honest students, who would never steal a candy bar from the college store or copy their neighbor's answer on a math exam, suffer an extreme temptation at this point or slightly after. Why not fudge a bit on the thesis? I could make my main clause say, "Civil disobedience . . . is unjustified," and then I would have the *instrument of good* term left over to make into a *because* clause! Alas, no. It is sometimes difficult to remember, in the search for a thesis statement, that one's ultimate object is a paper. A paper written from a "stretched" thesis statement simply gasps and dies at the point where a legitimate *because* clause belongs.

I must also beware of the *because* clause which is really circular. "Civil disobedience . . . is justified only when that government and its society cannot be expected to bring about

Getting a Thesis

more good than bad, *because* one ought never abandon an organization that can do good." What I have done in this *because* clause is to repeat the main clause in a more abstract fashion. Again, its inadequacy will become immediately apparent when I attempt to write the paper. At best, I will have one section of the paper simply repeating, in other words, what has already been asserted in another. And I will have an instructor wondering about me.

There is nothing for it but to confront seriously the question, "Why should one give up one's allegiance only in such extreme circumstances?" If this *why* question should prove unanswerable after forty-five minutes of hard thought, I will try to approach it in some other way. Perhaps I can make it more concrete. What situation can I imagine which would be a real parallel? A living group might work. Let us suppose that I live in a fraternity or cooperative which does something of which I disapprove. Let us suppose that it expels someone unjustly. In the first place, I would be obliged to argue against that action as vehemently as I could; that goes without saying. But let us suppose, further, that the matter came to a vote and the person were expelled in spite of my arguments. I would then be confronted with a new situation; according to my thesis I would have to decide whether that organization were still capable of a substantial amount of good. If I decided that it wasn't, I would have no problem. I would resign. But what if it still seemed to me useful? Why not resign anyway? That is my question.

In this concrete situation, I find that the *why* question about my thesis is indeed answerable. It would be foolish to withdraw from an organization still capable of a substantial amount of good because such a withdrawal would prohibit my being useful through that organization. And if I return with this general answer to the question of civil disobedience, I would find that it satisfies me. Once I withdraw my allegiance from a government, I would no longer be able to use that government, in however small a way, to accomplish anything worthwhile. In the context that Thoreau wrote in, having withdrawn his allegiance on the issue of the Mexican war, he necessarily abandons both government and society. There is no reason for either one to be concerned about his opinions on slavery, for instance. His possible usefulness in that matter is thereby nullified.

At this point, I am in a position to declare my whole thesis statement:

> Civil disobedience, with its attendant withdrawal from society itself, is justified only when that government and its society cannot be expected to bring about more good than bad, *because* otherwise the withdrawal of allegiance would nullify my own possibilities for doing good.

Now I'm elated by that peculiar sensation of "that's it!" Of course, I think, for who would want to spoil his own chances of doing good? Why, the whole point of the sort of civil disobedience which Thoreau recommends is to make one's life into a real force for the good. Yet it seems clear that such behavior can be expected to have just the opposite result. Unless the situation has become so desperate that one can no longer honestly expect good to prevail over evil in the community, that sort of total defiance would only be self-defeating.

This progress is rather satisfying. Not only have I come to recognize far more clearly what had bothered me all along about Thoreau's position, but also I have come to a more definite understanding of where I stand on the question. More than that, I believe I can say exactly *why* my own stance is more acceptable. The process of internal dialogue has revealed the basic ground underlying my conviction. Thus, I am now conscious of the general principle or major premise implied in my thesis statement. The notion that an individual's capacity for doing good should not be limited by his own actions surely would be acceptable to my audience, the writing class; a person who did not accept that wouldn't be concerned about civil disobedience in the first place. Apparently, my thesis statement has passed its big test. It does not seem to assume any more than my audience can be expected to take for granted.

Presumably, the actual writing of the essay could get underway now. After all, the really hard part seems to be over. I have arrived at a thesis statement which looks sound, and the chief task of my essay will be to explain the connections among its terms. Since my thinking has discovered those connections, that shouldn't be too difficult. Yet as I am glancing over the crucial terms with a view toward writing, I begin wondering. The whole thing now seems so obvious that it hardly needs to be pointed out. How could Thoreau have failed to see that? And what about all of those in class discussion with whom I was arguing the other day? Surely they must recognize that utter defiance of their society and its government is a measure to be engaged in only when the situation has become truly desperate. However, I know very well that neither they nor Thoreau see it that way. But why don't they? Since these are the very ones whom I must try to reach in the essay, I have to understand their point of view.

Such an understanding will require a kind of mental effort which I have not undertaken so far. Somewhere along the line, in working out my own position, I had entirely forgotten my prospective audience. A careful re-examination of that thesis statement is required, and this time I must have my audience firmly in mind:

> Civil disobedience, with its attendant withdrawal from society itself, is justified only when that government and its society cannot be expected to bring about more good than bad, because otherwise the withdrawal of allegiance would nullify my own possibilities for doing good.

Now the question is, what element in this statement will incur the most resistance from them? If I make a minimal effort to consider it from their point of view, I won't have to look very far or very long. The definitive phrase, "with its attendant withdrawal from society," must be the real pivotal point. The entire issue actually seems to turn on the belief, which my audience does not share, that civil disobedience amounts to a virtual abandonment of one's society. Unless I can get them to see that, my position won't be understood. So then, my main effort has to be concentrated toward getting that crucial point across. But why am I so anxious to make that point? Here I undergo a mental somersault. Suddenly, my thesis statement looks topsy-turvy. No wonder, for it is truly jumbled.

After all, what is it that I am concerned to prove? When I initially hit upon what I distrusted about Thoreau's conception of civil disobedience, what was I really after? Of course, I was trying to understand *my reason* for not thinking myself obliged

Getting a Thesis

to resort to civil disobedience whenever my society's government pursues a policy which morally offends me. Thus, my main idea is that there is something wrong about such behavior, however honorable may be one's intentions. But *what* is wrong with it? Obviously that it can spoil one's own chances of accomplishing any good. Yet although my thesis statement contains this thought and also a hint about the reasoning which underlies it, the content of the statement is curiously muddled. My main claim is down in the *because* clause, while its *reason why* is lurking in a parenthetical phrase in the main clause. Now, under my present critical gaze, that main clause seems rather hazy.[2] As a matter of fact, it doesn't say very much. And it seemed significant to me only because of my "insight" into the nature of civil disobedience which it implies.

So my thesis statement, which at first had seemed sound, has proved to be something of a logical mess. Still, it is clearly not to be abandoned as a total loss. Garbled as it is, the statement does express my essential thought. Actually, in discovering its muddle, I have also found the remedy. I merely have to unscramble my thinking and state it more exactly. And this I can do at once. The *because* clause must become my main clause, a statement of my thesis; whereas my conception of civil disobedience as a total abandonment of society will have to be my *because* clause, expressing my reason why. Thus, the reformulated thesis statement will read:

> Civil disobedience, in a society wherein good can be expected to prevail over evil, actually nullifies one's own possibilities for doing good, *because* such an activity constitutes a complete withdrawal from society itself.

That says what I had really meant all along. This revised statement more definitely expresses my position by accurately indicating the logical connection of the ideas involved. As a consequence, it renders the true burden of my essay much clearer. A brief inspection reveals that my audience will not boggle at

---

[2] A writer should always be wary of a thesis in which the verb "to be" plays the central role. It tends to a vagueness that does not help the writer find the precise relationship among his terms. Usually when that verb appears in the main clause of a thesis statement either the subordinate clause merely repeats the former in other terms or the main idea of the writer gets buried in the subordinate clause.

the general principle assumed here, which could be stated as "one can't accomplish any good through a society without being a participant in that society." Naturally, I shall have to work very hard to get my readers to understand and accept the notion put forth in the subordinate clause. But if I succeed in driving this point home, the assertion of the main clause will logically follow for them and they will understand why civil disobedience is a last resort to be engaged in only when their society is in really desperate straits.

At last, I seem to have the thesis statement I want. But how did I manage to miss it before? I'm curious about the puzzling thought process which has led me this far. As I look back, I can recall the anxiety in which my search for a thesis began. The class discussion had put me in a rather defensive frame of mind. "No," I remember having almost screamed at one point, "I wouldn't put women and children in gas ovens if my government ordered it, *but.* . . ." But what? That had to be answered. Thus, the need for justification was uppermost in my mind. So anxious was I to find the reason for my reluctance to embrace Thoreau's doctrine of civil disobedience, in spite of all the objections and rhetorical questions which had been hurled at me in the class discussion, that I temporarily lost sight of the exact question which had to be resolved. The disagreement has not been over whether or not one ever should engage in civil disobedience. Rather, the dispute boils down to whether such defiance would be an appropriate response whenever any action of one's government seems to be morally misguided. In formulating my original thesis I didn't have this question sharply in focus, mainly because I was so concerned to declare that there certainly were circumstances in which any person should defy his government. Now when the thought concerning the essential interrelatedness of society and government struck me, I experienced a great sense of relief. That idea seemed to settle things for me. Yet I didn't know how. For, since the real issue had become somewhat obscured, I failed to perceive its true import.[3]

But through a reconsideration of my initial thesis statement,

[3] Beginning writers frequently run into such trouble when they become disturbed by the question "Why?" before they have carefully thought out *what* they think in response to a specific question or issue.

Getting a Thesis

with a view toward my prospective audience, I was able to get the point at issue into clear focus. Once this perspective was attained, the weakness of the statement became manifest and I saw how to refashion it into this more adequate expression of *what* I think and *why:*

> Civil disobedience, in a society wherein good can be expected to prevail over evil, actually nullifies one's own possibilities for doing good, because such an activity constitutes a complete withdrawal from society itself.

Now after breathing a sigh of relief, as I consider what a travesty of my own position I might have produced had I remained in my previous state of confusion, I begin to think of translating this new thesis statement into an essay. Yet, in mulling the whole thing over for a bit, I decide it would probably be best not to set about that just now. It may be a good idea to let the problem lie for a while and become involved in something else.

When I come back to my thesis statement, perhaps the next day, it still appeals to me. In fact, I'm really beginning to like the sound of it. A fairly decent paper can come out of this, I feel. And yet, at the same time, there's something still bothering me. Somewhere in the back of my mind something is stirring, and I find that I can't quite shake the sensation that perhaps I have not really dug deeply enough.

Does this statement say exactly what I mean? Could it be made more precise? It seems to ring true, but I wonder. Well, one could brood like this for hours and still not get anywhere. Then I must quit *brooding* and start *thinking* again. Now is the time to push the crucial terms of one's thesis statement really hard, in spite of one's strong reluctance to do so. Their meanings and supposed connections must be probed further.

Perhaps I can better test my terms by actually imagining myself trying to explain them to my opposition. I know by now that considering those with whom one disagrees can help somewhat to clarify one's own position. By going further and trying to anticipate the kinds of objections they might raise, maybe I'll attain even more clarity. So, with my memories of class discussion and Thoreau's text before me to guide me, I decide to push on.

My notion is that since civil disobedience is an abandonment of one's society, it necessarily destroys one's own possibilities for accomplishing any further good through that society. Thoreau, of course, talks as if one could renounce his
allegiance to the government and still remain a genuine participant in society. As he says, very revealingly, "I am as desirous of being a good neighbor as I am of being a bad subject." And his persistent picturing of society and government
as wholly separate things shows how crucial that separation
is to the maintenance of his position. His argument clearly
could not be managed without it. For only by maintaining a
total divorce between the two can he insist on looking at government as a kind of alien force which does almost nothing of
any worth, and yet continue appealing to his neighbors as a
member of their community. In my view, however, Thoreau is
proposing an impossibility. Government and society, though
certainly distinguishable, are not totally separable. After all,
the government is really our way of ruling ourselves as a
society. So my conclusion still appears unavoidable. How in
the world could anyone . . . ? But wait; it can't be so obvious.
There's something behind Thoreau and the others' tendency to
see the matter so differently from me. What is it?

Well, what objections would they make to my line of reasoning? I glance through my pages of notes, and then begin
thumbing through the text. I have trouble, however, deciding
what I could or should be looking for. Besides, by now I have
become so distrustful of Thoreau that none of his words seem
to make much sense. This is no marvel, since I keep reading
only those passages which I marked when I first thought I
had found what was wrong with his view. Since my mind has
started to revolve in a closed system of its own, I really need
a talk with someone else—preferably with a classmate who
doesn't usually see things my way.

So that our story may have a happy ending, let us suppose
that the sought-for conversation proves fruitful. Suppose that
my view meets this kind of resistance:

> "You make it sound as if civil disobedience were an
> attempt to do away with society and government alto-
> gether, which is hardly the case. No, the idea is not to
> abolish the government nor to abandon one's society

Getting a Thesis

either. Rather, civil disobedience is a means for bettering both of them. It is an attempt to help assure that good will continue to prevail over evil, if you will.

"Isn't your fraternity example beside the point? After all, one can't resign from society itself the way one can cancel his membership in some club. The only way one could withdraw from his society would be to leave it for another society or, perhaps, some deserted island. And you were saying that Thoreau's conception was too simple! Instead of deserting one's society, civil disobedience means remaining and resisting the evil policies of one's government in the hope of effecting salutory change. It is having the courage to stay and stand up for what's right.

"Of course, our government has its virtues. Who would deny that? I'll even grant you, if you like, that it tends to accomplish more good than bad. But it can and does make grievous mistakes, as you well know. Are you going to stand by and let it proceed, without lifting an effective finger, when it perpetrates any serious evil?

"Now don't give me that stuff about using legal channels. As Thoreau points out, that may not be enough. Ideally, perhaps, ours is a government 'of the people,' etc. However, in actual fact, those who govern and the governed are not the same. And thus it can happen that those in temporary power can misuse their position to perpetrate a wrongful course without consulting the people beforehand.

"To be sure, under our system of representative government, no governmental policy can proceed very long if the weight of public opinion is overwhelmingly against it. But the general public tends to be lethargic. Civil disobedience is a way of alerting public opinion, of awaking society's moral sense when nothing else will work. It is a direct appeal to the consciences of others.

"Why do you want to insist that civil disobedience should be engaged in only when the situation has become so desperate that armed revolution might be necessary? Or isn't that what your position really comes to? Don't you see that such a nonviolent protest may be a way to help prevent things from becoming so desperate?

"The point is that some things are a matter of conscience. And any government, even one based on majority rule, may act in an unconscionable way. By and large, perhaps, the recognized processes for reform are fairly reliable. But they are no guarantee against immoral or unjust governmental policies. Majorities are not infallible. Sometimes the people themselves may be so misguided

Getting a Thesis

that all reasoned appeal through the 'public forum' may prove ineffectual. Civil disobedience is surely justified when other means can't be expected to be effective.

"You seem to think that once one has refused to co-operate with his government on any important issue he thereby forfeits all right to be heard by the society. But why shouldn't society and its government be concerned with the opinions of those whose moral convictions are so powerful that they are willing to run great personal risk in their defense? After all, the willingness to take such risk issues from a profound concern for the fate of us all."

Having heard all this out, I emerge in a rather unsettled state of mind. Much of it seems to make a good deal of sense. Indeed, seen in this light, why shouldn't one resort to civil disobedience when there's no other way? What could be wrong with that? Perhaps Thoreau and the others have been right all along.

But then why am I still reluctant to embrace their view? For something still disturbs me about the idea that one should refuse to support his government in any way whenever it behaves immorally in a matter of importance. But what precisely? I don't know, I guess the self-righteous tone of the whole thing annoys me. Besides, there seems to be something slightly incongruous about demanding that one behave morally instead of expediently and at the same time insisting that one do whatever he can to force his own convictions on others. Yes, that may be the crux of the matter. For when is civil disobedience said to be necessary under our form of government? Apparently, only when one's disagreement with the government's policy is not shared by most of the community. Otherwise, civil disobedience would not even be a temptation.

Well, then, my thinking hasn't really been off the mark at all. Since our government actually is the structure through which we as a community reach and implement decisions concerning our common well-being, a total refusal to support the government is at the same time an opting out of the community itself. It is to say to the society as a whole that one is so at odds with it that he will no longer participate in it. And, in my view, that does mean that he no longer has any right to expect either society or its government to be concerned with

Getting a Thesis

his views. I certainly would not take such a step unless I were convinced that my society and its government were mainly perpetrating evil.

Thus, once more, I find myself restricting the justifiable use of civil disobedience much more strictly than Thoreau and others. However, while the point at which a moral man ought to refuse allegiance to his government remains the same for me as before, I now see further into my real grounds for drawing the line there.

I not only understand more clearly the common ground which I share with Thoreau and those who agree with him, but also I recognize more exactly what divides us. We obviously agree in desiring as fair and as just a society and government as is humanly possible. And we seem to share the common belief that such a possibility depends upon a genuine respect for men's consciences. However, contrary to them, I do not think that civil disobedience fosters our common ideal. Instead, in my opinion, to engage in it on the conditions they maintain is to endanger seriously the very ideal they hope to promote.

That is what has really been behind my feeling that one who withdraws his allegiance from his government in protest of some "morally mistaken" policy can no longer rightfully demand that his society respect his views. That is an unfair demand because in refusing to recognize the government he is thereby refusing to respect the opinions of his fellow citizens. Which means that he is doing what he can to undercut the very possibility of having a fair and just society.

At last, I see where I stand and why. I now have a thesis statement which goes to the root of the matter:

> Civil disobedience jeopardizes the chances of maintaining a reasonably just community *because* such a refusal to abide by the collective decisions of the community necessarily involves a basic disrespect for the consciences of others.

The major premise involved here—"mutual respect for one another's conscience is necessary to having a just community" —obviously will be taken as self-evident by my prospective audience.

Getting a Thesis

Comment

As was said in the beginning, the working out of a thesis statement is a creative act. It is the work of an individual. Hence the above thesis statement is mine, not yours. The question proposed by Thoreau's essay can be responded to in many different ways. I have responded to it in my fashion.

What the student needs to observe is the kind of process involved in creative thought. It is not a methodical consideration of all of the elements in a situation. A great many possible questions were never raised in the search for a thesis statement represented in the foregoing. At no point was the nature of the good really considered, for instance. It was irrelevant to this thesis, as it turned out; but someone else's thesis might have hinged on that particular definition. The creative thought of the writer is a search or a pursuit. Its end is precision, not inclusiveness.

Conclusion

The writer of argumentation begins with an opinion about a subject. That opinion will invariably be too vague to form the subject of a paper. The first necessity is that he become precise in his thinking. He must become involved in a search ending in a discovery of the thesis which, in some peculiar way, was implicit in the original opinion.

This search for a thesis must be both aggressive and honest. It must also be flexible. When one line of inquiry dries up, the writer must be adaptable enough to change directions by asking himself another question. There are four general approaches to any problem which he can consciously bring to bear.

> 1. The problem can be analyzed to see if a specific kind of answer is required. Particularly, the writer should examine the problem to see if he does not need some criterion of discrimination. In the development of the thesis statement we have been considering, for instance, the basic problem was to find some criterion by which the writer could decide, "Here civil disobedience is justified; here it is not." Most human problems require such a criterion.

2. Careful definition of terms frequently leads to important insights into one's opinions. Such definitions are particularly useful when one seems to be going in a circle.

3. The writer should habitually look for concrete examples or analogies. "Do I know anybody who acts on that opinion?" "Have I ever been in or observed a situation analogous to the one I am considering?" All serious human thinking is rooted in the concrete instance, because it is in terms of the concrete instance that the individual must act.

4. A *why* question, earnestly answered, always moves the writer to a more fundamental level of thought. This is the most difficult maneuver of all, but it must be attempted a half-dozen times in working out a serious thesis statement.

The writer who is working out his opinion without reference to a text will ask these questions of himself. But when he is working from what someone else has written, these questions are equally appropriate to that other point of view.

The student will have observed, also, that the writer must make a great effort to maintain his involvement in the dialogue from which the question arose. In the search for a thesis traced in this chapter, the student insensibly drifted out of that dialogue as he pursued his own conviction. But he did not finally understand his own position until he returned to the dialogue by trying to imagine the response other students might make to his thesis. It is difficult to retain a sense of the opposing point of view while one is laboring to clarify one's own, but it must be done. The student who has a friend or friends holding a contrary opinion is fortunate.

The intellectual process described above is not an easy one. But there is no help for it; thinking is hard work. It has been the experience of the writers of this book that the rewards are commensurate with the effort required. A genuine thesis statement permits writing of a wholly different order than most students are accustomed to, and this purposeful, orderly writing is very satisfying. But, even more. We have never encountered a student who, having worked out a genuine thesis statement, did not find the effort in itself sufficiently rewarding, even if no paper were to follow. On one subject, at least, that student knew what he believed, why he believed it, and the consequences of that belief.

Getting a Thesis

4 | WRITING AN ARGUMENT

It cannot be said too often that any kind of writing is an act of communication and that, at some level, it aims at persuasion. An argument, particularly, is not written to be enclosed in a missile and shot off into space. Nor should it be written as a demonstration of proficiency for a teacher whom one is trying to please and not persuade. Ordinarily, it should not be written for a teacher at all. A student paper ought to be a piece of communication which the teacher has intercepted, in all kindliness, in order to improve upon its communicative efficiency.

The difference between an act of communication and a public declaration of feelings is that the former has an audience as a part of its essential character. Without some sense of whom one is writing for, decent writing is impossible. In the first place, the writer must have some sense of audience to feel the possibility of persuasion. He does not try to persuade the world at large; he attempts to reach this or that group or this or that person. Furthermore, what goes into an essay, detail by detail, can be determined only by some feeling for what one's audience already knows or will accept without proof.

For the experienced writer, the matter of knowing for whom he writes is a major problem; he never knows his audience well enough. The student can usually manage this problem satisfactorily if he will take class discussion seriously enough to enter into it. Ideally, a class discussion does not merely force the individual student to define his own position; it forces him to define it with respect to another opinion, or opinions, with which he disagrees. This awareness of opposition to one's own opinion is the reason for writing in the first place, and for the student it can provide a sufficient sense of the audience for whom he writes. Those classmates with whom he disagrees are his audience.

Writing, like thinking through a subject, is a kind of process. It will be useful to follow this process through the stages it will take.

THE INTRODUCTION   As previously noted, the actual writing of the essay can begin only after one has come to a clear intention. The thesis statement discovered in the previous chapter can serve to illustrate the process. The writer wants to persuade a particular audience having an opinion of its own that "Civil disobedience jeopardizes the chances of maintaining a reasonably just community." This thesis is the ultimate goal of the essay. When the student feels that he can assert it convincingly to his audience, the paper is finished. Thus, the task of the paper is to lead readers to the thesis as clearly and directly as possible.

But the first necessity is to find some starting place, to discover a point from which movement to the thesis can begin. Furthermore, this starting point must appeal to as many readers as possible. The function of an essay's introduction is to fulfill these two necessities. An introduction seeks to establish a point of departure which will seem promising to prospective readers.

There is no unique introduction for a given thesis; any thesis can have a variety of starting points. But they will all have one characteristic in common. All of them will try to

Writing an Argument

involve readers in a particular problem to which the thesis is supposed to be an answer.

Only by raising a real question in such a way as to convey a sense of urgency about settling it can the writer secure a foothold with his audience. At the very least, then, his introduction must focus reader attention upon a definite issue. And it must do so immediately. Dawdling here will be self-defeating. No writer can afford to keep his readers wondering for very long what might be on his mind. He must put the object of his concern before his readers as quickly as he can if he wants them to continue reading.

But how does he go about raising a real question, issue, or problem? It might seem that the student who has gone through the agony of thinking out a precise thesis statement which says what he thinks and why would not have much trouble at this point. After all, such a statement could have been reached only through an attempt to resolve some question which had disturbed him. The proposition that "Civil disobedience jeopardizes the chances of maintaining a reasonably just community" was finally discovered as a response to a problem with which the student had been struggling since the class discussion of Thoreau's essay. Consequently, he must be thoroughly familiar with the problem he wants to lay before readers in the introduction.

Yet when it comes to the actual writing of the essay, the introduction may well be the hardest part. Several temptations may beset the student which, if not firmly resisted, will prevent him from doing his best. It is very easy, for instance, to become overly anxious to declare one's answer. This tendency seems to be particularly hard to curb. Beginning writers frequently feel impelled to announce their thesis right away before they have suggested the questions that the thesis answers. This temptation stems perhaps from a discomfort with the whole persuasive enterprise.

If the writer's object is to persuade, it is a strategic blunder for him to begin with a proclamation of his thesis. In the first place, a statement is, as a rule, less interesting than a problem; hence the declaration of his thesis in the introduction will lessen reader interest. Second, if the reader does not immediately assent to it, he will perhaps resist unduly whatever reasoning may be put forth later in support of it. Actually he may not even bother with what follows. Third, a thesis statement in the introduction simply puts the writer at the wrong end of the stick, and invariably he must scrabble awkwardly from the end of his argument back to the beginning before the argument itself can begin. Finally, it may be observed that again and again students who put their thesis at the beginning— because no one likes to repeat himself and because the thesis statement has already been proclaimed—get hopelessly lost and write very bad essays about something other than they intended.

Closely allied with the temptation to begin with a bald assertion of one's thesis may be a tendency to feel that the question is so obvious that one need only ask it point blank. Undoubtedly it has become rather obvious to the student by now. But he cannot afford to presume that the particular problem which concerns him will as a matter of course equally concern his audience. While the question which he wants to resolve arose from a class discussion of some text, that does not mean that his classmates see the question in just the same way he has come to see it. Actually, the disagreement which he has been having with some of them may hinge in part on the way the question itself is construed. As a matter of fact, if the student thinks back to his own struggle to find an adequate thesis he will recall that it was not always easy to keep his mind focused on the exact question which he was trying to answer. That memory in itself should be enough to make him realize that he must define his question as precisely as possible for his audience.

If thoughtfully considered the experience of class discussion will assist the student writer immensely with the task of the introduction. As has been said, his confrontation of other points of view there provides him with an invaluable sense of his audience. If he will bear in mind the opinions of those who disagree with him, he will keep alive that tension and urgency from which his thesis statement originated. In this way he will be less apt to lose his opportunity for writing persuasively in the first paragraph by yielding to the temptations just mentioned.

By now it should be evident that raising a real question

Writing an Argument

does not mean merely telling the reader that there is a very important question which should be discussed. The point is to *show* the reader that there is a genuine issue which needs to be resolved and to interest him in an attempt to resolve it. The introduction must reveal that the writer is sensitive to the serious difficulty involved in settling the issue in which he wants to engage them.

Furthermore, the issue to be argued must be raised in a way that will establish a point from which the writer can lead his readers to the conclusion he wishes to urge. That is, the introduction must in some fashion lead to a step of the argument by which the writer hopes to secure assent to his thesis.

Let's see in concrete terms how this initial task of the essay might be accomplished. The thesis "Civil disobedience jeopardizes the chances of maintaining a reasonably just community," it may be remembered, was conceived as a response to the question "Should one resort to civil disobedience whenever his government pursues a policy which outrages his moral sensibilities?" There are several possibilities for raising this issue in an interesting fashion. Since the student's thesis was developed in response to Thoreau's affirmative answer to the above question, one possibility which immediately presents itself would be to begin with a vivid and concise statement of Thoreau's view. The introduction thus developed might be called a *some say* introduction.

> Thoreau, in his essay "On the Duty of Civil Disobedience," insists that one is obliged to put up effective resistance to one's government whenever it pursues a morally evil course. In such an event, he says, it is not enough to petition the government or to engage in other legal methods of protest. If one is sincerely and deeply convinced that the government is acting immorally in a matter of great importance, one cannot in good conscience rest content with such feeble expressions of dissatisfaction. "Cast your whole vote, not a strip of paper merely, but your whole influence. A minority is powerless while it conforms to the majority; it is not even a minority then; but it is irresistible when it clogs by its whole weight." Thus does Thoreau enjoin us to withdraw allegiance from the government and refuse to support it in any way in an effort to combat its wrongful course. In

his view, there is no other alternative for a truly conscientious citizen who really desires justice to prevail. Since only a fool utterly lacking any moral sense would contend that our government never does anything seriously wrong, there is hardly anyone who could remain utterly aloof to this stirring appeal. Human nature being what it is there are bound to be times when each of us finds himself morally disturbed by some governmental action. Obviously, at such times one is obliged to bring his concern to the attention of the government and the citizenry it represents. And traditional democratic processes of decision-making are likely to seem terribly slow then. So that, obligatory or not, civil disobedience can seem very tempting.

In a *some say* introduction the writer defines his problem by setting up a point of view which is different from his own, but which can yet function as a point of departure for his own point of view. The material following the quotation suggests to the reader that perhaps Thoreau's answer is inadequate.

An alternative to *some say* is the *funnel-shaped* introduction in which the writer begins by setting up a very large question, presumably one of interest to his audience, and then progressively narrows it to the specific problem he has proposed for himself. Given the same thesis as above the writer might set up the problem as follows:

The true hope for a democratically governed society has always lain with responsible and vigilant private citizens. For, while much less liable to abuses than dictatorship, representative democracy is by no means immune to abuses of power by those in authority. Thus if genuine human values are to be preserved, there have to be individuals willing to criticize the government whenever it acts in a way that will endanger any of those values. Perceptive exercise of the individual rights of petition, assembly, freedom of speech, and freedom of press is, of course, the traditional safeguard against such abuses. And ideally that should be enough. But in actuality it may not be. It is entirely possible for a democratic society to become so morally corrupt or indifferent that it will allow those in power to perpetrate the most inhuman of atrocities. An overwhelming majority might, for instance, choose a Hitler. Given such a situation, the only recourse for a moral man would be a complete withdrawal of allegiance from that society and its government. It would be fatuous to maintain that one should support that government merely because a majority of the people approved of it or acquiesced in it. But need circumstances be so desperate in order for civil disobedience to be justified under democratic rule? Even supposing that one's government by and large is an agency for good, might not one be justified in defying it to the point of civil disobedience whenever it is guilty of a serious moral transgression? Couldn't such an action be seen as a legitimate extension of the traditional democratic rights of protest?

Notice how the writer progressively zeroes in on his specific question. He begins by affirming the importance of the traditional forms of protest in a representative democracy and quickly passes over the general question of whether civil disobedience is ever justified in order to set up the real issue to be resolved. Observe in particular the progressive narrowing of the question in the last three sentences.

One further kind of introduction might be illustrated, in which one defines the problem by rejecting or modifying the terms which might commonly be used to discuss it. This can be called a *selective* introduction:

In quarrels over civil disobedience, one frequently hears such phrases as "law and order" and "individual conscience" juxtaposed as if they were polar opposites. Thus it seems that there are two different kinds of people: those who believe in laws and those who believe in the consciences of individuals. One would think that it is impossible to believe in both. Yet surely the question of whether a man ought to protest a morally objectionable action of his government, be it a legislative enactment or an executive decision, is itself a matter of conscience. And as such it can be decided only in direct personal terms. Above all, one has to remember that this decision has to do with real persons and not abstractions. For what one has to decide here is what sort of relationship with others should he seek?

It should be pointed out again that the three examples above do not represent all possibilities. They are simply three ways of establishing a position around which the writer can rally his readers and from which he can lead them to the point he wishes to make. The student is perhaps better off if he does not consciously select a particular strategy at all. But he must define a problem to which the thesis is an answer and he must make an attempt to interest readers in that problem. Every argument is persuasory.

THE BODY OF THE PAPER   It has been pointed out that a precise and concrete thesis statement constitutes a kind of goal, a point to which the writer proposes to guide the reader. But a precise thesis does much more. It lays out the steps the writer must take in order to move from his introduction to a declaration of his thesis. All communication, beyond a cry of pain or pleasure, depends upon the establishment of a particular relationship among concepts. *"Death of a Salesman* is not a tragedy," "The UN preserves world peace," "Love transcends class"—each statement proposes that a certain relationship exists between two terms. A precise thesis helps the writer to establish this relationship directly.

One can begin to consider the problem posed by the body of one's paper, consequently, by simply making a list of the terms which might enter into an exposition of the thesis. For the one worked out in the previous chapter the list would be:

> Civil disobedience
> jeopardizes the chances of maintaining
> a reasonably just society
> because
> necessarily involves
> basic disrespect
> consciences of others.

In other words, the student begins by listing terms and relationships. "Civil disobedience" is a term, a subject. Verbs and conjunctions propose certain relationships between the subject and the other terms of the statement. The paper will not deal with all of these terms; in the act of writing the student will discover that certain of them have self-evident meanings

Writing an Argument

in the proper context. Very often a term and a relationship will be handled at the same time, but it is a good idea to list everything.

The act of writing, then, will be the act of linking these terms and relationships meaningfully. There is no way of determining in advance the order in which they will be most effectively linked. The one rule is that the writer cannot follow the order of the list. His intention is, after all, to join "civil disobedience" to "a reasonably just society" in a particular way; if he were to follow the order of his list he would accomplish this junction without including his *because* clause in the paper. This consequence is obviously undesirable. Perhaps the most common pattern is to begin with the subject of the main clause and end with its object, linking them by means of the *because* clause elements, but this is by no means a rule to which the student should appeal.

Nor is a rule necessary. If the thesis is a substantial one and if the student really wants to persuade, writing the body of the paper is the easiest part of the whole task. Students frequently find that it takes at least ten or twelve hours to discover what their thesis is. It may then take an hour to write a one-paragraph introduction. Frequently, the paper can then be completed in less time that it took to write the introduction.

But where to begin? The answer is, "Where the introduction has brought you into the problem." For instance, the *some say* introduction proposed earlier (page 48) would lead, obviously, into a consideration of civil disobedience, the first term of the thesis, as would the *funnel-shaped* introduction which follows it. The *selective* introduction, on the other hand, naturally sets up the object of the *because* clause, "the consciences of others."

The ordering of elements is usually not a problem in the writing of an argument; it is, in some sense, "natural." The introduction sets up one of the thesis elements as the first term to be considered in the body of the paper; that first term will set up the next one. The student usually knows what is to follow the paragraph he is writing before he is halfway through it.

How this works can be illustrated by actually writing the thesis which has been considered to this point. A different in-

Writing an Argument

troduction, it will be noted, brings the writer into the thesis statement at still a different point from those set up by the introductions already proposed as illustrations.

Proponents of civil disobedience sometimes are misunderstood as anarchists who want to abolish society and government altogether. Yet it is clear that their intention is much less alarming than that. Actually the true aim of civil disobedience is not to undermine one's government, but to improve it. The hope is to arouse the conscience of the community against what one perceives to be a pernicious governmental policy. It is supposed to be a personal kind of protest appealing directly to the moral sensitivity of one's fellow citizens. Hence, we need to consider the nature of this kind of protest in order to judge it fairly in terms of its own explicit intention.

This paragraph resembles superficially the selective introduction previously examined. However, it has a different purpose. The writer begins by correcting a common misinterpretation of civil disobedience, one that would prohibit any effective discussion of the subject if left to stand. He then proceeds to place the subject in a light which permits it to be considered intelligently.

It will be observed that this particular introduction leads the writer very easily into a definition of the first term of his thesis. In the introduction, "civil disobedience" was used in a general way, as the manifestation of his intention. But the general meaning of the term is not sufficient; in the second paragraph it must be defined in a fashion useful to the writer and acceptable to his audience.

The first thing to remember is that civil disobedience, though definitely and intentionally disruptive, is nonviolent in character. It is essentially a direct attempt by concerned individuals to stymie a particular governmental policy which they consider morally repugnant by simply refusing to cooperate with or support the government in any way. By totally withdrawing their personal allegiance to the government, the protesters hope to rally further opposition to the abhorrent policy and bring it to a halt.

Obviously only a great sense of urgency could prompt anyone to resist his government to the point of civil dis-

Writing an Argument

obedience, since such a complete withdrawal of allegiance from one's government involves considerable personal risk. And naturally, those who do not share one's own sense of urgency about the matter are apt to be alarmed to find one openly refusing to support the government even in a passive way. But, then, that is precisely the point of this type of protest. One needs to resort to it only because most people in the society are not morally appalled by what the government is doing. For if the majority seriously objected to the policy, our democratic government could not continue to pursue it. The intention is to shock the rest of the society into a recognition of the evil which at the moment is recognized by only a minority.

Thus, civil disobedience could be justifiable only as a last resort. No conscientious citizen would seriously consider engaging in it until he had earnestly availed himself of the traditional processes of democratic dialogue. Only after petitioning, speaking, and writing at some length have proved ineffective in changing public opinion should the possibility of civil disobedience tempt him.

The introduction of this essay led directly into the term "civil disobedience." But this is a rather complicated term and the writer finds that he has to handle it in stages. In the first paragraph he explains *what* kind of protest civil disobedience is. In the second and third paragraphs, he specifies the *when*, *where*, and *why* of it. Notice that the third paragraph logically could form a part of the preceding paragraph, since what it says, that civil disobedience is justifiable only as a last resort, is implicit in the assertion of the previous paragraph, that it arises in a sense of urgency. But apparently the writer sensed a need for setting the point apart for emphasis. This kind of emphasis is usually a sign that a significant shift is about to take place. In fact a shift of tone has already begun to show up in that third paragraph. The verb "tempt" is revelatory in this respect, although the shifting began some sentences earlier.

How long is one supposed to attempt to explain his conviction before he decides that it is time to adopt some more effective means? If the intention really is to appeal to the consciences of one's fellow citizens, can this be done by renouncing the government?

Writing an Argument

Since, under our representative democracy, the government is simply our means for arriving at and implementing decisions concerning our well-being as a community, it is hard to see how one could renounce the government without renouncing the community itself. But this fact makes the supposed moral commitment of civil disobedience, to say the least, very ambiguous. One simply cannot renounce others and expect to continue appealing to them on moral grounds. The government and the majority which supports it can be expected to do only what they believe is right. And when one honestly thinks that they are seriously mistaken about that, then one must seek to change their minds. But this can only be done by entering into dialogue with them, reasoning with them, and appealing to their human sensitivity.

Clearly, civil disobedience is not and cannot be such an appeal, because it constitutes an absolute refusal to abide by those procedures for adjudicating differences of opinion upon which the possibility of dialogue rests. Those who resort to civil disobedience are really saying that they are weary of trying to explain their point of view and that they think further discussion useless. In essence, then, civil disobedience is a declaration that one no longer considers the rest of the community to have any genuine moral sense to which one might appeal. It is a proclamation to the effect that one has given up on them as human beings deserving of respect.

These last three paragraphs attempt to establish a connection between the first term of the thesis statement, "civil disobedience"—the subject of both the main and subordinate clauses of the statement—and its last term, "disrespect for the consciences of others." The essay is now approaching its conclusion, since all that remains to be done is to relate this third term to the second term, "jeopardizes the chances of maintaining a reasonably just society."

Naturally, faced with such a declaration, the community can only respond by treating the individuals issuing it as enemies. Thus, if a sizeable minority were to defy systematically the legal procedures of decision-making, they could succeed in so polarizing the society as to make the entire process unviable. Consequently, one should weigh and consider the issues very carefully before allowing his impatience with others to get the better of him. By succumbing to such impatience and destroying the possibility of further dialogue with other citizens, one could endanger much more than his personal well-being.

Ultimately one has to decide where his commitment really lies. If he sincerely wants to see justice prevail he has to ask himself how he must live in order to help bring about this goal. Thoughtful men have always looked upon the process of democratic dialogue as the best means of assuring that men can live justly and fairly together. It is based on the faith that through a mutual respect for one another's consciences men can arrive at reasonably just decisions concerning their destiny together. While this process of dialogue may seem slow and painful, especially when it doesn't seem to be going in the direction one feels it should, it is still the only truly human way.

Thus in the end the matter boils down to what kind of attitude one adopts toward those with whom he lives. No doubt he may consider them and their elected representatives to be seriously misguided at times. But are they always or usually committed to an immoral course? No doubt, if one really thinks that most people in the community are so morally deranged that further appeal to their consciences would be pointless, one would have no other course but to sever his ties with them completely. Unless that were the case, however, one would only jeopardize the chances of maintaining a reasonably just community by following such a course.

The conclusion, it will be noted, is simply a restatement and elaboration of the main clause of the thesis statement. This is the statement to which the whole essay has been directed, and it seldom presents a problem if the thesis has been honestly conceived. (The *because* clause may or may not be included in the final paragraph; it is neither required nor out of place.)

Comment

A good thesis statement does not set up a formula for writing an argumentative essay. It defines the purpose of the essay and indicates the steps which may have to be made in order to argue the thesis effectively. The writing itself is still a creative act. In fact, by requiring that he undertake all the hard, conscious thought first (in the formulation of his thesis statement), this approach to writing can in fact make the creative act possible.

There are several general observations about the act of writing which might be mentioned at this time, although several of them will be considered in greater detail in the next chapter.

1. The thesis statement does not provide an outline; in fact, an outline ought to be avoided. It is sometimes helpful to jot down important subpoints under particular thesis terms and relationships as these subpoints come to mind. But a formal outline can look very logical and right and prove, in the writing, to be impossible. The process of writing must be in part a process of improvisation.

2. It is perhaps an exaggeration to say that the best paper is one that is written in the least time, but it is a helpful exaggeration. The first writing of the paper ought to be fast. When the paper loses its impetus, the student should not labor with it. He should, instead, look for drastic remedies. The first, and most drastic, remedy to be considered is reordering. Is there some more effective way of reordering the elements of the thesis statement?

3. When his ordering seems inevitable and the paper still drags, the student should look to his topic sentences. The topic sentence is a kind of basic guide for the whole paragraph. If it is loosely formulated or if it is off the point, the paragraph will begin to drift. When it has drifted very far, it will stop dead. Do not spend a lot of time on limp sentences in the middle of a paragraph; reconsider the topic sentence instead. If that doesn't help, go back to the topic sentence of the previous paragraph.

In short, a paper ought to move. It is ordinarily moving satisfactorily as long as the writing seems to have some life of its own. When the life suddenly disappears from the writing, either the elements of the thesis statement are in the wrong order or bad topic sentences are pulling their paragraphs out of line.

To the student accustomed to giving three reasons for a very vague and casual opinion, the procedures for getting from opinion to an argumentative essay indicated in this chapter and the previous one may seem very time consuming and difficult. They are both. But the serious student will find the effort worthwhile. In the first place, if the student takes the pursuit of a genuine thesis statement seriously, he will discover (and not invent!) important opinions which he can now understand and articulate, whereas in the past he could only point vaguely to important feelings.

Second, the finished product may resemble the kind of work a professional writer does. It will be governed at every step by a very specific persuasory intention. Furthermore, it will move steadily toward the realization of that intention. Writing will become a creative activity.

STYLE | 5

Style is a word which is, at best, slightly alarming to students—and with reason. What does it mean? Sometimes it seems to mean something like "fancy writing." "This paper is not very interesting stylistically." More often, perhaps, it is used in a context in which it is a property of the student himself. "Your style is pompous," or "Your style is cluttered up with too many subordinate clauses." My style? I didn't even know that I had one. And if it is pompous, it is going to have to stay that way; I don't know what to do about it.

Yet both kinds of comments reflect valid and useful ways of considering style. Value judgments are appropriate to style, although "fancy" isn't an appropriate value judgment. And style is a quality of the writer. Both kinds of judgments can be illustrated from the following passage by a contemporary naturalist: [1]

---

[1] Loren Eiseley, *The Immense Journey* (New York: Random House, Inc., Vintage Books, 1949), p. 26.

Men talk much of matter and energy, of the struggle for existence that molds the shape of life. These things exist, it is true; but more delicate, elusive, quicker than the fins in water, is that mysterious principle known as "organization," which leaves all other mysteries concerned with life stale and insignificant by comparison. For that without organization life does not persist is obvious. Yet this organization itself is not strictly the product of life, nor of selection. Like some dark and passing shadow within matter, it cups out the eyes' small windows or spaces the notes of a meadow lark's song in the interior of a mottled egg. That principle—I am beginning to suspect—was there before the living in the deeps of water.

There, we sigh, is style.

But wherein lies its felicity? This is a difficult matter for even professional critics to be specific about. We can start by observing that the style does not exist apart from what is being said. In fact, we respond to this passage as being particularly notable for its style precisely because that style is at least as important for communication as the paraphrasable content is. What the passage says, to paraphrase it brutally, is that the organization of living creatures, as this might be described by scientists, is perhaps inherent in "the deeps of water"—a very mysterious possibility. The function of the style is to make the reader *experience* that possibility. The passage is about "organization," a sufficiently scientific notion. But "organization" is balanced throughout the passage by the mystery, by "fins in water," by "dark and passing shadow," and so forth. In short, the function of this style is to balance two ways of looking at nature, in a fashion that preserves for the reader the validity of both.

Every style does not aim at a balancing of opposites, of course. But we can say that every style incorporates *a way of relating to* the particular subject. It will be useful to call this relationship between the writer and what he wants to talk about his *stance.*

Stance is not peculiar to essays; something analogous is habitually operative in our daily behavior. I may be straightforward with one friend and ironic with another; at times I am very much in earnest and at other times I am playful. We do not have a vocabulary to specify these different attitudes with precision, and so they are difficult to talk about. But we are aware of them in other people and perhaps even in ourselves.

Stance is this sort of attitude-taking manifested in style. Some sort of stance is always present in prose simply because we must have some relationship to what we are talking about; that particular stance is appropriate if it helps the writer accomplish his ends.

But the style of the above passage does more; while it defines *stance* it also tells us something about Professor Eiseley. The student who is not aware of the writer as at the same time a gentle and thoughtful man, possessed by a kind of passionate reverence for nature, should read the passage again. And the style makes us aware of this personality. But we must be wary of assuming that Professor Eiseley is simply this kind of man. For one thing, it is quite likely that Professor Eiseley does not always write like this; it is likely that he writes at times in a "professional naturalist" style quite different from this one. So it would be inaccurate to say that the style reflects the personality of the writer. Let us say instead that *a style reflects those elements of the writer's personality which are appropriate to his persuasive intention in that particular work.* Again, a term will be useful. Let us say that this second major function of style is to create an appropriate *ethos*.

In short, the major functions of any style are to create a *stance* appropriate to the subject under consideration and an *ethos* appropriate to the persuasive intention of the writer. These are created by the same means and hence they are difficult to keep separate, but the student will do well to think of style as embodying two distinct, if not separable, functions.

There is no mystery and nothing to fear in our consideration of style up to this point. The particular writer is a human being writing for other human beings, and it stands to reason that he will be present, in some fashion, in his writing. He will be present in its style. We also know that the cliché, "it all depends upon how you look at it," embodies enduring truth. A blackbird seen head-on is a different object from a blackbird going away, and the writer, no matter how much he would like to, cannot present his subject from every possible angle. Writing necessarily involves a particular perspective—

Style

one way of looking at the subject among a number of possibilities. This perspective, too, is at least partially a matter of style.

But where do we look for the style? That is the scary question. Because, of course, it is no place and every place. Style is not a matter of diction, or sentence structure, or ordering. It is the whole thing. Let us, for example, rewrite Professor Eiseley's first sentence: "Ever since the time of Darwin, men have talked of nature as matter and energy and the struggle for existence." But this would not do. The whole paragraph would have to be rewritten had Professor Eiseley begun in this fashion. (As a matter of fact, the whole book would have had to be rewritten to get in such a sentence!) We have changed a half-dozen words, altered the sentence rhythm, and utterly transformed the style of the sentence. But, given the pervasiveness and complexity of style, how is the student expected to manage it? There is, it seems, no place to begin.

But of course there is. Professor Eiseley began someplace. We have insisted throughout this book that the model for the student of writing must be the professional. So far as style is concerned there is no alternative. How does the writer skilled enough to be paid for it establish and control style: that must be our question.

STYLE AND EARS   It is perhaps the case that the mass civilization of the twentieth century tends to diminish individual differences. But at most this is only a tendency to be measured by comparison with earlier ages. On the other hand, it is a fact of everyday experience that the individual is recognized by those around him as a distinct personality. Personality is not just something that charms other people, although it may do that too. It is a characteristic way of seeing the world and responding to it that, for other people, adds up to a coherent individual. It is what we are interested in and value; it is the way we ordinarily respond to experience; it is gaiety or gravity, openness or reserve, commitment or scepticism. It is what we are.

This personality (which itself is a kind of life style) is the only possible basis for writing. The student who finds himself charged with having no style is actually being charged with failure to express himself as an individual with a characteristic way of responding to the world. Style is not something that he doesn't have; it is something that he has excluded from the writing process.

Nor does this mean that the student need undergo a series of personality tests in order to work out a style. "It says here I'm witty—hmm, maybe if I put a joke in. . . ." No, no. We have said that personality, or life style, is manifested in our behavior, and perhaps most clearly in our verbal behavior. What we are, our personality, is reflected in the kind of words we use, our characteristic phraseology, the kind of comparisons we habitually make, and so forth. This personal voice is what the student must get into his written prose. This voice is the only possible source of a decent style in student writing.

To put it another way, the problem with style that the average student encounters when he begins to write is actually a reading problem. Few students have learned to hear inside their heads the words that they see with their eyes. One can read simple prose with one's eyes alone. But the fact is, no one can *write* prose of any kind whatsoever without the help of his ear. On the other hand, the moment the student begins to hear what he is putting on the paper—when he hears the pauses indicated by his commas, when he hears what an inversion does to meaning or how a particular word echoes another—his voice will be in his prose style.

The student who would really like to be able to represent himself on paper as literate will deal with this problem as one in reading. He will make a habit of reading aloud, particularly those passages which seem to him obscure. He will shortly find that much prose which he had found too difficult presents no difficulty at all when read aloud. He will even find comprehension and pleasure in poetry if he permits himself the experiment. And he will at the same time collect a supply of stylistic options for his own prose.

But the student need not go so far to get some sense of himself into his prose. He need simply labor with his prose sentence by sentence, reading it out loud and trying to transcribe exactly what sounds best, in order to begin learning the

Style

relationship between what he hears and what he writes. In so doing he will simply be imitating the habitual practice of the professional writer.

It is our experience that for most college students sufficient attention to the aural dimension of their writing guarantees at least stylistic adequacy. Written prose is not speech, but they will find that they also have in their heads the conventions of written prose which enable them to translate speech into prose style without much conscious concern for the problem.

Of course hearing what he writes will not solve all a student's writing problems. Spelling, particularly, is only roughly phonetic in English and some faculty in addition to ear is required for its mastery. It is unfortunately the case that twelve years of almost daily classes in spelling do not assure the acquisition of that faculty; intelligent and zealous college students may be abysmal spellers. It is perhaps grossly unfair of twentieth-century society to estimate a writer's intellectual capacity by a faculty which seems to have been left to printers a couple of centuries ago.[2] But the writer, as we have pointed out, chooses to communicate and must take his audience as he finds it. He must do what he can about spelling. If the value of the dictionary is limited for him because he doesn't know what to look up, he needs to find his own version of the seventeenth-century printer—a friend who has mastered this vulgar but necessary art.

Nor do we all have in our heads equally acceptable models of English prose style. These models are a kind of residue from our reading, and the individual who has not done much reading, or whose reading has been eccentric, is certainly handicapped in a writing class. It must be added that, in our experience, one seldom encounters in college a student whose prose models are disastrously inadequate.

In any case, there is no other place to start. On the most elementary level, we must hear a pause in a sentence, for instance, before we can worry about what rule is to be applied

2 One of the curious facts in the history of orthography and to a lesser extent grammar generally is that by the beginning of the seventeenth century printed texts were highly regular: there was a correct spelling for each word, a correct mark for a certain length pause, and so forth. On the other hand, most manuscripts written in English were chaotic in these respects. The inescapable conclusion is that the printers introduced the regularities which today are demanded of educated men.

to indicate that pause—whether we need a comma, semicolon, or whatever. (With some practice in listening the student will soon find that his ear not only signals a pause but dictates the length of that pause to most people's satisfaction.) As for style above the level of grammar, there is simply nothing other than his own style available to the student, and this style becomes available only through listening to his own prose in a fashion analogous to the way he listens to his own voice in ordinary speech: [3]

The student must be cautioned again, however, that spoken and written discourse draw on different conventions. At the very least, written discourse must be more economical than conversation or even formal public speaking. The student's problem is not to reproduce his spoken vocal patterns on paper but to adapt those patterns to written discourse, which has its own conventions.

WHAT ONE LISTENS FOR   It has been pointed out on many occasions in this book that the student needs no direction as long as his writing is moving along briskly. This principle is especially applicable to stylistic matters. If the student can hear with pleasure, or at least without pain, what he has actually written, he should carry on without undue concern for unperceived stylistic lapses. The student whose prose models are inadequate can learn to listen for certain kinds of stylistic defects, although this kind of learning is laborious.

1. *Unfunctional sentence distortions.* The student has been told often enough that he should not write subject-verb-object sentences exclusively because they are monotonous. They are worse than that; they are hypnotic. But deviations from that order ought to be functional; they ought to represent the intention of the writer more precisely than normal order would. What a sentence finally means is a matter of weight as well

[3] It is useful to get into the habit of hearing what we write literally—by reading aloud as we write it. But we should also learn to hear entirely within our heads, to feel the relationship of words to each other without the intervention of the physical ear. How we are able to do this can be left to the psychologists; we need merely cultivate a faculty obviously available to us.

as a matter of relationship. "The writing itself is the major fault of the work" does not say quite the same thing as "This is the major fault of the work, the writing itself." The second sentence is a lot more emphatic than the first by reason of the displacement of its real subject, "the writing itself," from its normal order to the end of the sentence. Only context could determine the preferable form, but the use of one form where the other was appropriate would be a stylistic fault because there would be some kind of unintentional discontinuity between that sentence and its context. In short, variations in word order affect meaning.

But it is very easy for the instructor to say too much, in too general terms, about the relationship of word order, or whatever, to meaning. In one of the famous passages in literature, Jonathan Swift, arguing ironically that we should always content ourselves with the surface of things, writes.

> And therefore, in order to save the charges of all such expensive anatomy for the time to come, I do here think fit to inform the reader, that in such conclusions as these, reason is certainly in the right, and that in most corporeal beings, which have fallen under my cognizance, the outside hath been infinitely preferable to the in; whereof I have been farther convinced from late experiments. Last week I saw a woman flayed, and you will hardly believe how much it altered her person for the worse.[4]

By all the rules of sentence structure this passage is simply awful. Swift obviously was not bent upon saving anybody money, and yet his first phrase by its emphatic position flaunts this as his motive. The way the first sentence is broken up by phrases and clauses ("that in such conclusions . . . reason . . . and that . . . which have"), by arresting us in our search for the meaning of the sentence, makes the final object very emphatic, and proves to be a truism. But Swift was not yet content; he portentously promises us an example of his truism, and it turns out to be that a woman who has been skinned is altered in her appearance. And then he must add "for the worse"! Swift was not after the effect envisaged by rules of sentence struc-

---

4 Jonathan Swift, "A Tale of a Tub," *Gulliver's Travels* (New York: Modern Library, Inc., 1931), p. 475.

ture; he was a great writer because he made up his own rules in accordance with his particular ends.

The point is not that the student should write like Swift; it is that he should evaluate what he has written against what he intended to say, not against some vaguely remembered rules. It is perhaps necessary in learning to write that we learn rules of writing. But at some point they become a positive hindrance, at least psychologically.

2. *Controlled movement.* We have insisted upon movement in writing until the student is probably sick of the subject. No matter; it is the essence of the craft he proposes to learn. As readers we expect a new sentence to incorporate some sort of advance in thought while maintaining a solid connection with the sentence which has gone before. But—of course—not all of the time. There must be leaps in argumentation as in narrative writing. The student needs to become sensitive to the function of the leap as well as the more common progression. Henry Adams illustrates the leap nicely: [5]

> Until the Great Exposition of 1900 closed its doors in November, Adams haunted it, aching to absorb knowledge, and helpless to find it. He would have liked to know how much of it could have been grasped by the best informed man in the world. While he was thus meditating chaos, Langley came by, and showed it to him. At Langley's behest the Exhibition dropped its superfluous rags and stripped itself to the skin, for Langley knew what to study, and why, and how; while Adams might as well have stood outside in the night staring at the Milky Way.

The leap here is in the third sentence. Adams dramatizes the change in direction rather than attempting to conceal it, as he balances "showed it to him" against "meditating chaos." But the leap of the sentence is a genuine one; the prose moves from this point in quite a different direction from the one it was taking earlier. There are two principles necessarily involved in the management of prose movement at this level. (1) Be sure leaps of thought are clearly signalled. (2) Don't signal a leap unless there really is one.

[5] *The Education of Henry Adams* (Boston: Houghton Mifflin Company, 1961), p. 379.

Style

3. *Balance of parts.* The student needs to approach this consideration gingerly. Every grammar book cautions against repeating oneself. This is by and large a useful caution against the pernicious impulse of the neophyte writer to paraphrase what he has just said while he tries to think of something to say next. But it is at best a partial truth, as witnessed by the fact that the person giving the advice usually violates the principle in the very act of enunciating it. ("Do not repeat yourself. Say what you have to say clearly the first time, and move on.")

The fact is that meaning in an essay is in part a matter of relative weight. A point which is developed through three paragraphs is by that very circumstance understood by the reader to be more important than a point succinctly presented in one. But it is a further fact of everyday experience that the importance of a point to an argument bears no necessary correlation to the amount of time and effort it takes to make that point clearly and convincingly. It is quite possible that I could lay out the subject of an essay very adequately, as far as meaning and persuasion are concerned, in one clear and forthright sentence. If I do so I run the risk of being totally misunderstood. I must weight that subject with amplification, proof, and so forth, which the subject considered by itself does not require but which are required by the essay as a whole to create a proper balance between the subject and the other elements of the essay.

This is probably the first time this observation has been made to freshmen, and we make it with some trepidation. The beginning writer is apt to err on the side of unnecessary amplitude, and we would not encourage that vice. But weight is an element of meaning, and no one intent upon the craft of writing should be unaware of that fact.

4. *The stylistic break.* Perhaps the most common purely stylistic failure in student writing is the sentence that is open to gross misunderstanding. Very often it is a joke or a piece of irony. The obvious inference, when one's choice humor comes back scored in red, is that certain normal human faculties, like a sense of humor, are lacking in the scorer. But this is not a necessary inference. What has happened, almost invariably, is that the student has violated the *stance* and *ethos*

Style

already established. One defines oneself for the purposes of the paper in the introduction. Any attempt to become something else thereafter, unless the writer is very skilled indeed, simply leads to confusion. One dare not permit a sentence in the body of the paper which could not have been written by the person defined in the introduction.

5. *Repetitions.* To repeat a word even once in a passage gives it perhaps three or four times its normal emphasis. The professional writer uses this device habitually; famous passages in English prose may repeat one word a dozen times in a half-dozen sentences. But an accidental repetition has precisely the same effect as a deliberate one, with unfortunate consequences. One needs to learn to listen for nonfunctional repetitions as well as to manipulate functional ones.

6. *Awkwardness.* It is the writer's responsibility to organize the words that he uses into phrases, clauses, and sentences in such a fashion that the reader is never even momentarily at a loss. "Every word in its place, and that place obvious": this is the ideal. It is of course an impossible one. Even the best writers fail. Let us look again at the passage by Loren Eiseley offered at the beginning of this chapter as a model paragraph:

> Men talk much of matter and energy, of the struggle for existence that molds the shape of life. These things exist, it is true; but more delicate, elusive, quicker than the fins in water, is that mysterious principle known as "organization," which leaves all other mysteries concerned with life stale and insignificant by comparison. For that without organization. . . .

Wait a minute. No one can read "for that without organization" in this context without stumbling and rereading.

We are obliged to regard this as a venial fault because we are nervously certain that the instructor could illustrate the same sort of slippage from this present book. But fault it is, nonetheless, and something to be avoided. Professor Eiseley undoubtedly heard the offending sentence with a heavy accent on "that," but there is nothing in the position of "that" to indicate on first reading that it requires such an emphasis. We deduce such an emphasis on second reading because meaning, not position, requires it. But a second reading shouldn't be necessary.

The last stylistic flaw illustrates very happily the necessity for an editor. Professor Eiseley in reading the passage gave "that" the emphasis required for meaning without realizing the reader had no reason to emphasize it; a sixth reading on his part might not have uncovered the difficulty. Even one reading by a stranger to the text would have suggested that there was a problem. "For that without organization" would simply have proven too big for his mouth as he tried to get the words into a meaningful relationship to each other. There could be a meaner basis for choosing a friend than the ability to simply read aloud what is written on the paper. The writer then need merely listen for signs of distress on the part of the reader and in every instance honor that distress by revising.

THE INTRODUCTION   We have been considering the general problem of style as the reflection of the individual in the prose he writes. But there is more to style than this; there is the question of its suitability to the particular job at hand. In our daily lives we are sometimes witty and sometimes utterly without wit, depending on the circumstances. As writers we need a similar flexibility. In other words, the voice in style is not simply a matter of imitating one's ordinary, conversational voice. It also reflects a particular *stance* and a particular *ethos*, as we have pointed out. How does the student manage these?

The writer's definition of himself, his *ethos*, and his relationship to his subject, his *stance*, need to be approached in two quite different ways. In the body of the paper *ethos* and *stance* may present no particular problems, but this is true only if the writer has been very much aware of *ethos* and *stance* as he wrote his introduction.

In every way, the introduction of an essay is the most difficult part of it to write and very often takes the most time. As was pointed out earlier, the introduction must define the question of concern to the writer in a way that will lead into the body of the paper, and it should be so written that it engages the attention of readers in that question. In addition, the writer must define himself in some fashion on this first appearance and he must set up an attitude toward his subject. In short, the introduction must establish *ethos* and *stance*.

The student will perhaps be surprised to learn that the joy in writing is to be found in the more complex responses to these dreadful necessities. But in an informal way the student has probably already discovered for himself the fun of playing with *ethos* and *stance*. The letter home in which he sets up a kind of parody of himself to whom funny things happen—that is an *ethos* game. And the conversation in which he disconcerts friends by adopting an eccentric position toward a subject—here he is playing with *stance*. There is no reason why these complexities should be forbidden in more formal communication. But there is, alas, a priority to be observed. The first order of business must be to manage the straightforward and relatively uncomplicated *ethos* particularly associated with argumentation and the *stance* that goes with it. With luck, there will be time later for fun and games.

THE
MINIMAL INTRODUCTION

Let us say that I want to make a particular point for a particular audience. Because the audience is a group of my peers—a writing class—the problem of relating to them is minimal, and I have no reservations about the point I wish to make. What must the introduction do to make persuasion possible? In the first place, it must establish me as a reasonable, trustworthy sort of person. Few people are willing to listen to cranks, and we are suspicious of a position on anything which might be described as eccentric. Next, the introduction should make the audience comfortable. An audience which is nervous is not listening closely. Finally, it must set up the problem in a straightforward fashion. How do I go about incorporating these attitudes in my introduction?

Experience has shown that the student who is involved in his subject and at all aware of his audience will set up an introduction containing these types of *ethos* and *stance* without paying too much attention to them *if* he can avoid certain common hazards. His problem is negative, in a sense; he must not make those moves that will wreck the *ethos* and *stance* which are normally there and quite adequate to his needs. The most common mistakes of this sort in student writing are:

1. *Shrillness or excessive vehemence.* The writer must trust his audience to respond with the proper degree of concern for the problem presented. The inexperienced writer often lacks such trust; he attempts to force an adequate response by being exclamatory. "Surely every loyal American wants his country to be victorious no matter what!" Such a sentence demands that the reader respond. And ordinarily he does—adversely. He concludes that the writer is an unreasonable sort of person who is trying to trap him into some position that is probably also unreasonable, and he stops reading.

2. *Inflation of the problem.* This habit again reflects a distrust of the reader; the writer, to be sure of getting attention, overstates his case. "The one great decision that every human being must make. . . ." Even if the the writer thinks that this is a literal statement of the fact, he is better off not to declare it so baldly, particularly in his introduction. We are more apt as readers to trust someone who understates the gravity of a situation than someone who overstates it.

3. *Excessive generalization.* This fault is related to the one above but arises from a different motive. It is the statement which could not possibly be supported in the first place and which is irrelevant in the second. "Men, ever since the dawn of history. . . ." The student who makes such a declaration is simply not paying much attention to what he is saying. He has fallen into the *stance* of the Fourth of July orator. The reader who does not like fireworks will abandon the essay in favor of a peanut butter sandwich, never to return to it.

4. *Apologetics.* As was pointed out in the earlier chapters, no sophisticated reader will regard any essay as God's last truth upon the subject. The writer has an opinion which he thinks is true and worth the attention of the reader. That is the only claim that he makes, and that is all the reader wants of him. Hence there is no necessity to apologize for intruding oneself on the reader's attention, nor is there any necessity to point out that other opinions exist unless it suits one's own strategy to do so. The student who insists that his opinion is imperfect, tentative, contradicted by other opinions, and perhaps utterly in error merely invites the reader not to read.

Style

There is a good deal of misunderstanding among students about this writer-reader relationship. When the writer introduces "In my opinion," "I think," and similar phrases into a text, he does not implicitly claim that anything not so introduced is undeniable fact. Such phrases are signs to the reader. They merely indicate that the writer does not want his whole argument to be judged on the basis of the statement that follows the "I think." Ordinarily such phrases are used to introduce material relevant to the argument but not necessary to it.[6]

5. *The windup.* As has been pointed out, the writer works from the thesis statement, which is to be developed in the body of the paper, to the problem, which will be set up in the introduction. For one reason or another the student sometimes begins too far from that problem. If the problem of the essay is civil disobedience, there is really no need to consider in the introduction its history or its relationship to the two-party system. The problem needs to be formulated by the writer as crisply as the thesis statement itself was formulated; otherwise his introduction is apt to give the impression of a writer looking for something to say.

If the student can avoid these common mistakes and other less frequent ones, the introduction should adequately define an *ethos* and a *stance.* However, this will happen only if his introduction is adequate in the first place. The following paragraph is simply not an adequate introduction:

> Thoreau's essay, "On the Duty of Civil Disobedience," argues that whenever we disagree strongly with what the government does we are obliged to withdraw our allegiance from that government. Of course, there are a lot of people today who agree with Thoreau. But I think he was wrong.

What such a poverty-stricken introduction tells the reader is that (1) the subject isn't very interesting, (2) the writer

---

6 "I think," if repeated several times can have quite the opposite effect from the one described here. "I think the prisoner sneaked into the bedroom of the deceased; I think he stood behind the door while the deceased dozed before the TV; I think. . . ." The effect of these "I think's" is to challenge the reader or hearer and to demand more certainty of him than would be demanded if the "I think's" were not there.

doesn't really care what his audience thinks (this kind of indifference is insulting), and (3) the writer is a slob. *Stance* and *ethos* there is aplenty in this kind of meager writing, but not of a very desirable kind. In fact, they are always present in persuasive prose, and the writer who neglects them will suffer for that neglect.

THE OPEN STYLE   There is one further consideration about the introduction that is worth the neophyte writer's attention. Since it concerns characteristics of style which are very difficult to talk about, two illustrative paragraphs will help to make the point:

> Writers concerned with allegiance have habitually thought of the problem as writers; they have considered what relationship a writer should bear to the state. But a writer has peculiar relationship to the rest of society. All his activities are at least potentially public, because his profession gives him access to public attention. Hence when he elects civil disobedience, his action is consequential. But the person who is not a writer must recognize that an act of civil disobedience on his part will not be consequential. He must, therefore, justify that act in terms that entirely personal.

This is an adequate introduction. It sets up a problem very straightforwardly. The *ethos* is that of a writer who is serious, thoughtful, and eminently reasonable.

The second introduction sets up very much the same *stance* and *ethos*, but it adds another, and oftentimes useful, dimension to that style.

> Writers concerned with a problem are like other human beings; they think of that problem with reference to themselves. Thus, when they worry about the proper relationship of the individual to the state they think about the proper relationship of the writer to the state. But the writer's relationship to anything is peculiar. All of his activities are, in some sense, public, or he can make them public if he wants to. Hence when he elects civil disobedience, his action is consequential; a large number of people are going to read about his reasons for

Style

such an election. But the person who is not a writer must recognize that an act of civil disobedience on his part will probably not be consequential. Civil disobedience wears a different face for him and must be justified on different grounds.

Most critics would describe the difference here as one of tone. The first paragraph establishes a level of formality and maintains it within very close limits. The second paragraph even uses sentences from the first, but it opens downward, toward conversation.

Both kinds of tone—all kinds of tone—have their proper uses in different contexts. But the student will usually find the openness of the second an advantage. Having established this openness he can go to the formal style in the high points if he chooses, and he can treat other matters with a lighter hand.

THE MORE COMPLICATED INTRODUCTORY STRATEGIES The word that one uses, one's sentence rhythms, the way sentences are balanced against one another —in short, style—are obviously a part of the art of writing and not of its craft. The student's intuition must provide the appropriate diction and his ear must select the appropriate rhythms. The teacher cannot tell him how to do these things. Even the minimal introduction finally depends upon the student's intuition.

The student who would aim at something beyond what is required in a writing course can be told this: nonnarrative prose is in almost all instances a practical activity; it is directed to some consequence. Style also is practical; it is not something added onto prose apart from the intention of that prose.

The question the student must answer as precisely as possible for himself is, "What do I want to do that cannot be done with the minimal style as defined above?" Almost always a prose style gets complicated for some sort of complexity or doubleness in the writer's intention. Professor Eiseley's style, for instance, creates a sense of mystery in nature; this is balanced against the surface nature as science describes it. This balance is the point of that style, the reason for its use.

Style

75

Most complex styles originate in some ambiguity in the writer's attitude toward his subject. A scandal in the athletic department, for instance, may be of some consequence; it may be worth writing about. But scandals in athletic departments are, at the same time, not of the first order of seriousness. A sophisticated writer thundering against overpayments to a left tackle would feel like a fool unless he could qualify his thunder by some indication that his perspective was not limited to problems of this order. And his qualification would be chiefly stylistic.

The writer should be as conscious of his own intentions as possible. In the above instance the writer would want to argue against a piece of local corruption. But he would also want to seem sophisticated to his readers—who presumably would themselves be sufficiently sophisticated to know the ways of colleges when first-rate tackles are in short supply. And in his introduction he would very carefully balance one intention against the other:

> Nobody supposes that football players from southern California migrate to Northern Minnesota Tech because they love snowstorms or because they want to major in forestry. The bronzed strangers who present themselves to the coach each fall must be presumed to have other, more private reasons. But those reasons ought to be kept within decent limits. Football is a game, and a game doesn't make any sense unless it is played with some reference to a set of rules. The rules of football prohibit the use of Sherman tanks, and they also prohibit salaries of $20,000 a year to left tackles.

This paragraph sets up a serious problem, particularly in sentences three and four. But the *ethos* of the paragraph is that of a writer who knows the ways of the world and does not overestimate the local college scandal.

THE BODY AND THE CONCLUSION OF THE PAPER   The student who has worked out a concise and pregnant thesis statement which pleases him and who has written an introduction which leads to that thesis statement with no discontinuities or strains has almost done the job. In many instances the main problem that the student has in writing the body of the paper is to keep up with the flow of ideas; he finds that he can think his paper through faster than he can write. He should write just as rapidly as he can.

But of course minor problems arise. A word doesn't seem like the right one or a sentence suddenly appears which is incurably awkward. The student must learn never to labor very long over such a specific problem. Because, almost always, it isn't *really* the problem. The real problem is in a larger structure. If the right word doesn't present itself within a couple of minutes, the problem isn't the word, it is the sentence. If the sentence can't be straightened out with a little tinkering, the student needs to reconsider the paragraph in which it occurs.

Fixing word problems by changing sentences is easy. The student need merely try it a couple of times and discover that it works. Repairing paragraphs is not so easy.

During the last couple of centuries, the paragraph has become in Western societies the basic unit of thought in writing, but it is a unit of thought with a conventional shape. Convention dictates that the first sentence be a topic sentence— that is, that it express in a general way the point of the whole paragraph. (If the writer does not want it to be a topic sentence he has to signal this fact to the reader.)[7]

---

[7] This chapter is an attempt to deal with writing problems as they can be expected to arise among college freshmen, and it is our experience that such students, writing from genuine thesis statements, seldom have difficulty with paragraphing. For the student who is curious about such matters, however, it can be pointed out that there are two variations to the paragraph structure described above. (1) A paragraph may begin with a transitional sentence when the writer feels the reader needs help in relating what is to follow to what has gone before. A transitional sentence is easy to spot. It is often a question: "But what is the value of such a distinction?" Or it says, "But we need to be careful in drawing this conclusion." The way that the sentence is framed indicates its transitional character, and the topic sentence can be expected to follow the transitional material. (2) Rarely, a topic sentence is found at the end of the paragraph. Usually this happens when the writer is afraid that his audience will resist the point he wishes to make. Hence he presents his evidence before he draws a conclusion from it. Again, this eccentric organization must be signalled. The first sentence will say something like "Let us take three examples of civil disobedience." This cannot possibly be a topic sentence nor can the examples which follow. The topic sentence will necessarily be pushed down into the tail of the paragraph.

It should also be pointed out that introductory paragraphs are a different enterprise altogether because they commonly move from one point to another to another. If they can be said to have topic sentences at all, these will ordinarily be found near or at the end of the paragraph.

Style

What follows the topic sentence will amplify, clarify, limit, or argue for the proposition made in that topic sentence. We learn to read paragraphs in this fashion. We hold the topic sentence in our minds and fit the sentences which follow to that proposition.

The topic sentence functions as a kind of control point for the writer. If the topic sentence says what he means clearly, the paragraph writes itself, very nearly. If the topic sentence is inaccurate or vague, the paragraph which is supposed to develop the proposition in the topic sentence will run into stylistic difficulties.

This point is a little difficult to illustrate, because paragraphs function in the context of other paragraphs. But let us suppose that the writer wants to make the point that civil disobedience involves the breaking-off of dialogue between the disobedient citizen and others; he comes up with the following paragraph:

> Civil disobedience, in a funny kind of way, is an appeal to force. What the citizen says by his actions is, "I will refuse to stay in relationship with you which permits us to talk together." Of course, civil disobedience is ordinarily associated with nonviolence, and the disobedient individual does not ordinarily use force himself. But his action is an invitation to others to use force. And of course. . . .

The student here is fighting his topic sentence, which does not say precisely what he wants it to. The further he goes, the vaguer his sentences get. The ready way out of the difficulty is to write a new topic sentence for the paragraph.

But what if the very worst happens and even a revised topic sentence will not get the paper moving again? It has been snapping along through four or five paragraphs and suddenly it grinds to a halt. One tinkers with the word, the sentence, the paragraph—nothing helps. The prose, which has been writing itself, gets hopelessly snarled and awkward.

The writer in this dilemma calls upon the same principle as before, the principle of the next higher unit. He has been working from a very roughly formulated list of the points to be covered, derived from his thesis statement, and any prolonged problem indicates that he has been working at the list in the wrong order. If the definition of civil disobedience, calculated for the third paragraph, doesn't write itself in that paragraph, then it probably ought to go somewhere else. Worse. If the third paragraph, for instance, is the point at which the writing stops, the basic problem is almost always earlier, in the second or even the first paragraph. The writer will save time by starting all over.

In short, there are two major principles to be applied in writing the body of the paper. Writing ought to be fast: that is the first major principle. The paper which, in the writing, is sticky and labored has something the matter with the conception behind the writing. The thesis is defective somehow or the order of the handling of the elements of the thesis is wrong. The student should always be trying to get the paper moving by understanding the problem. As long as writing is painful, it is bad. (Assuming, of course, that speed does not arise out of sheer innocent incompetence.)

The second major principle is that a writing problem is almost never where it seems to be. The writer must always looks to the larger context of a writing difficulty, and the quicker he looks there the less time he will waste. It is not easy to throw out a perfectly good paragraph because the next paragraph is sticky, but there is no point in delay. The principle of the next higher unit is finally almost infallible.

Little needs to be said about the conclusion of the paper. It is a restatement of the thesis. Since the thesis is the point at which the writer has been aiming all along, there is no problem in declaring it eloquently when he is finally in a position to do so.

The student is always encouraged to revise. A professional writer does not submit first drafts; it is arrogance when the writer who is not a professional presumes to do so. But the revision should be a very vocal process. The student should read the paper out loud to himself. He should try to make it sound as good as he can. Finally, he should get someone else to read it to him and listen carefully for the places where it is difficult to read. The function of this second reading is to make sure that the paper actually represents his own reading, that what his ear has told him is right is actually reproduced on the paper. If the paper sounds right to him when someone else reads it, the student has done what he can.

Conclusion

The student who has spent years with books on style is apt to wonder if it can be so simple a matter as it is represented to be here. But it is not a matter of style being simple; it is a matter of doing the best one can by using the proper instruments. Style is overwhelmingly a matter of voice in prose, and this voice is controlled by hearing it. The student's style—the flexibility and precision of his vocal patterns—may not be what he would like. But he will not improve it dramatically in a writing class. In the writing class his job is to get the best style available to him into the paper.

FROM ARGUMENTATION TO REPORTORIAL WRITING

The student who has written one good arugmentative essay has learned the most important principle of prose writing, the principle of movement. And he has learned it the only way it can be learned, by experience. In trying to keep up with the progress of his thesis from introduction to conclusion he has felt in some fashion the kind of impetus that good writing has. Through this experience he will have achieved a critical means of examining his own compositional structures. He will have discovered a test of effective prose that is very nearly infallible. He may thereafter write a defective argument, but it will be easier for him to see the defect and he will often be able to see its nature without being told in detail. He may still profit from a critic but he will no longer need a teacher.

But, as was pointed out in the first chapter, all writing is not argumentative. The student must expect to be asked to do other kinds of writing in his college career and afterwards. In the ordinary course of things he will not be asked to write poems, short stories, or novels. But he will be asked time and again to do reportorial writing. Therefore, he will need to transfer what he has learned in writing argumentation to reportorial writing.[1]

REPORTORIAL WRITING   As we have seen, argumentation is defined by the fact that it gets its structure from a thesis statement. To put it another way, argumentation joins two terms—the subject and object of the thesis sentence—by means of at least one more term introduced in the *because* clause. The writer of argumentation derives his organization from the fact that these terms already bear an essentially logical relationship to each other.

Reporting as defined in this book is best understood as writing which is engaged in presenting a single term. Both the writer of argumentation and the reportorial writer might have for a subject Thoreau's attitude toward civil disobedience. But the reportorial writer would not have a predicate for that subject, and hence he would not have a thesis.

Reportorial writing lacks predication because its aim is to convey information about a subject rather than to make a judgment about it. What is the situation in Vietnam? What is the state of the economy? What are the prospects of Reed's College's football team this season? Essays directed to questions of this sort will ordinarily be engaged in giving the reader masses of information bearing upon the question but will not have an argumentative thesis.

It can be seen that most of what we read in modern news magazines, such as *The Reporter* and *Harper's*, is reportorial, although one cannot assume this to be the case in a particular instance without examining the structure of the piece. In college, term papers are usually reportorial, as are most examinations. The student will seldom be in doubt about the kind of writing required of him: if the instructor wants information, he wants reportorial writing; if the demand is for evaluation or opinion, argumentation is probably in order.

---

[1] Frequently a writing class will never get beyond argumentation. The student need not be distressed by this. If he has learned to write an argument he can ordinarily transfer what he has learned to reportorial writing without the assistance of an instructor.

From Argumentation to Reportorial Writing

It should be pointed out that it is not the lack of opinion which is the mark of a reportorial writer, but the lack of a thesis as that was defined in Chapter 3. The reportorial writer is a human being with opinions, and like all human beings, he would like to see those opinions prevail. He differs from the writer of argumentation not in intention but in means. He chooses to persuade by amassing information.

Reportorial writing can be very complex. Most of the "kinds of writing" taught in a composition class, for instance—narrative, exposition, description, analysis—are really strategies available to the reportorial writer to accomplish specific ends. It is obviously impossible to illustrate all these complexities in this book. Nor is it necessary; the problems are much the same for reportorial writing no matter what the complexity. These can be sufficiently illustrated by considering what might be involved in writing an essay examination when the instructor has requested information. Thoreau's essay will again be a useful subject. How the process might be extended if one were fulfilling a more complex assignment, like a term paper, can be considered as we go along.

PRELIMINARY ACTIVITIES   When we undertake to write an argument, our chief effort must be directed toward the clarification of our thinking. But the emphasis in reportorial writing is on information and not judgment, and it follows that the writer must begin by collecting information.

Term papers can be fatally damaged by the way in which the student manages this first step of information-collecting. Many students assume that slips of paper inserted in a collection of library books are an adequate substitute for notes. The problem is that the information thus located is ordinarily being used by the writer of that book for his own purposes; it is imbedded in the movement of ideas in the book and is hence a part of its structure. The student working from an open book has a great deal of difficulty in resisting that alien structure. The sentence following the one he originally noted looks pretty good, and the one after that, and so forth. The term paper can only be incoherent as a consequence, because

From Argumentation to Reportorial Writing

no matter how well joined the ideas are in the book, they will not lead where the student wants them to. Worse, the student who gets careless is likely to find himself accused of plagiarism.

The mechanism of note-taking is very much a matter of taste. There are two general rules. First, each note should be on a separate piece of paper or an index card to permit easy manipulation of the information thus collected. Second, source and page number should be indicated for each note. The student who once spends a couple of hours trying to identify an insufficiently documented note will probably remember to identify notes thereafter.

The student taking an examination has no notes, of course, and hence has no such problem. But he has another problem. The student's impulse is to fill up paper, no matter what the instructor has said. But a preliminary process of gathering and organizing one's information is still the student's only warrant against chaos. At least one-third of the time available on an essay examination should be given to this preliminary process. In the examination, the enduring necessity that one think before writing presents itself to the student as a major test of his character. But no student that we have persuaded to restraint has ever been saddened by the result—a better essay.

Let us assume that I, as a student, have manifested character and that I have spent ten or fifteen minutes of the hour allotted to the examination in reviewing my information about "On the Duty of Civil Disobedience." I will have made a list of the points I remembered, which might look something like this:

> night in jail—interesting
> majority rule is matter of strength, not right
> soldier on parade is model of obedience
> voting not important
> problem is Massachusetts, not South
> merchants more interested in money than morality
> all recognize right of revolution, now worse than 1775
> government best which governs least
> have to be poor to be virtuous

From Argumentation to Reportorial Writing

one man can make a difference
object is justice, not expediency
opinion not acted upon doesn't count
government doesn't do any good
taxes is point where individual meets government
constitutional ways of changing take too much time
at least not support wrong

It will be noted that the entries are brief (very often one word will do) and that they are put down simply as they occurred to me. But there is enough information in the list to satisfy any instructor if I can get it into an examination in an intelligible form. (Had I begun writing immediately my paper would have been approximately as disorganized as my list.)

The student will observe that my procedure has not been different in kind from what it would have been had I been writing a term paper (or a reportorial article for *Harper's*, for that matter). In every instance one begins by collecting information. The requirements of an essay examination make that collecting somewhat less detailed and precise.

Nor is the process of organizing this information essentially different. Whether I am writing an essay examination or a book, I need to find a minimum number of *heads*—general principles or categories—under which my information or points, can be classified. The way to find such heads is to go carefully through the information collected and see what more abstract statements are implied in the individual points that I have jotted down.

There may be occasions when the writer simply makes up his heads: Thoreau's definition of the state; his conception of citizenship; and so forth. But he is better off if he can find his heads implicit in his raw material. For this reason the heads which emerge will vary widely in character, depending upon the kind of materials the student is attempting to organize. In a history examination, for instance, the chief heads could very well be four or five major historical events around which the lesser points might be gathered. In the present instance the heads will obviously be topical.

Let us start through the list. Why did Thoreau introduce the account of his night in jail? Surely to show the reader

From Argumentation to Reportorial Writing

that the consequences of civil disobedience are not so bad as he might think. We can set up "nothing to fear" as our first head. The second point, about majority rule, is a part of Thoreau's assault on government; we can title the second head "government not important." The third point, about the soldier, can be similarly classified, as can the fourth.

The student writing an examination needs to be quick about this process, of course. The most efficient procedure is to write the heads down separately, as they occur to him, preceded by "A," "B," "C," and so forth. Then, when each point has been given its appropriate letter, the information is classified sufficiently for purposes of writing an examination.

The writer working under more leisurely circumstances might retabulate his list to look something like this:

A. Nothing to fear
night in jail
B. Government not important
majority rule matter of strength, not right
soldier is model of obedience
voting not significant
government best which governs least
government doesn't do good
C. Individual should act
problem is Massachusetts, not South
one man can make a difference
All recognize right to revolution, worse than 1775
object is justice, not expediency
opinion not acted on doesn't count
taxes point where individual has to do with government
constitutional ways of changing take too much time
at least not support wrong
D. Individual's problem
have to be poor to be virtuous
merchants more interested in money than morality

I need to look at this grouping once again. Several questions ought to arise as I do. Both the first and the last heads are too short, but, on second thought, I can see the possibility of combining them effectively. Also, the point about the merchants might not be important enough to be worth mentioning in the paper. Finally, the point about voting not being very significant conceivably belongs under "C" rather than "B."

From Argumentation to Reportorial Writing

There is no need to resolve any of these questions at the moment, but it would be sensible to indicate them on my second list—to put arrows indicating the possible relationship of the first group to the last and to put a question mark by the point about the merchants and an asterisk by the one on voting.[2]

It should be pointed out that what I have *not* got is any sort of outline. I have, rather, a list of points to be covered in the essay which have been gathered roughly into heads. But beyond this gathering there is absolutely no order. Nor does the student need more order than that. He needs to find out where to begin.

THE STRUCTURAL PROBLEM IN REPORTORIAL WRITING   All essay-writing gets its structure from the fact that it is composed of units. But the heads of reportorial writing differ from the terms of an argument by reason of the fact that they are not linked to each other by anything more than a common subject matter. Furthermore, in longer and more complicated efforts this common subject matter may be very broad indeed. A comprehensive study of public housing in my home town, for instance, might include its history, the number of people availing themselves of it, income distribution in the population at large, the cost of public versus private housing, and a half-dozen other major heads. These heads would be related only by their common relevance to "public housing in X."

And yet the same obligation is on the reportorial writer as is on the writer of argument. He, too, has initiated this particular piece of dialogue, presumably because he cares about what his audience thinks, knows, or does not know. It would appear that his contract with his audience is the same as the contract of the writer of argumentation; it is a contract to get somewhere, to make all of these words add up to some-

---

[2] A student writing an examination will do well to get in all the information at his disposal. But in other circumstances, even reportorial writing is governed to some extent by structural considerations. A student writing a term paper should be prepared to find half the information he has collected excluded from the final paper because it could not be utilized without damaging the movement of the prose.

From Argumentation to Reportorial Writing

thing. His audience is as subject to boredom as any audience if it seems that the writer has lost sight of or abandoned that contract. In short, one would suppose that reportorial writing, no less than argumentation, must move.

Actually, it must *seem* to move. By definition, the reportorial writer has information rather than a thesis in mind, and the heads under which the information is gathered are related to a common subject matter but not to each other. Hence he has neither the intrinsic connections nor the conclusion upon which argumentative movement depends. But if he is skillful he can seem to have both. The art of reportorial writing is, in fact, the art of making pseudoconnections which will lead to a pseudoconclusion.

This is not to say that the genre is by nature immoral. The writer has information—presumably useful and accurate information—which his audience ought to possess also. His job is to present it in a form that is readable. But an essay which gets nowhere—which has, in fact, no place to go—is not readable. So the writer must invent what he doesn't have. He must impose a structure on materials which are not capable of an intrinsic structure.

If the student will examine a half-dozen reportorial essays attentively, he will discover that the reportorial writer ordinarily borrows his structure from one of two other genres, history and argumentation. In effect he organizes the material he wants to present by imitating the structure of one or the other. The procedures in the two cases are sufficiently different to require separate treatment, although our consideration of pseudohistory can be brief.

REPORTORIAL WRITING BY PSEUDOARGUMENTATION To this point I have collected the information which I propose to include in my examination essay and have gathered it into heads; I have three organizational elements to deal with instead of fifteen. Furthermore, I have resolved to write from an argumentative model. The first question to be asked then is, "Is there *any* way the heads can be related to each other?" I discover that I can combine these three heads into a statement very easily. I can assert that Thoreau argued, "although there are limitations and conse-

From Argumentation to Reportorial Writing

quences to such acts, the individual is obliged to acts of civil disobedience because the government is not important."

If I think about the essay for a moment, I will very quickly realize that I have stumbled onto something very like Thoreau's opinion about civil disobedience (it is too vague to be a thesis statement). Thoreau worked from opinion to supporting points, but I have gotten back to the opinion again through my attempt to organize those points.

This kind of coincidental discovery can be counted on to take place when the reportorial writer is doing an account of a body of materials—for all practical purposes, an essay or a book—which has been preselected by a human intelligence with a governing opinion. This fact can be a useful one. The student, being asked to give an account in an examination about "On the Duty of Civil Disobedience," for instance, knows in his bones that the teacher wants not merely information but some clue as to Thoreau's intention. He is very apt to be confused by the need to integrate the two in brief compass. But he has really no occasion to worry about it. He need merely proceed in the usual reportorial fashion by listing his points and gathering them into heads; if there is a governing intention in the body of materials he is being examined on, it will emerge.

But this kind of implicit relationship among heads is not to be expected in other writing situations. A writer will almost never have occasion to do a reportorial essay on another essay or book except in the artificial situation of the classroom. He will still need some integrating principle for his essay. Fortunately, a pseudothesis need not organize heads into a grammatical relationship with one another to be useful. What it must do is to set up a point of reference which will enable the writer to pass along information as though it were directed to a conclusion. "The Civil War had many causes." "Chaucer tends to use the same devices for humor in all of his late works." Perhaps the invariable mark of the pseudothesis statement is that it is not to be taken seriously in itself, usually because of its obviousness. It is an organizing device.

In any case, I have solved the problem of the body of my paper. In an examination I would probably write the body and let it go at that. But when time is not so limited the

From Argumentation to Reportorial Writing

writer ordinarily completes the illusion of argumenative writing by devising an introduction. Since this demonstration must stand for all varieties of reportorial writing, an introduction is in order here.

As a careful student I will have read the introductoy materials to the essay under consideration, and since, in this instance, the instructor is particularly concerned to evaluate the knowledge I have available, it would be very sensible of me to demonstrate my zeal by writing my introduction around these miscellaneous facts. It might go something like this:

> Thoreau's "On the Duty of Civil Disobedience" has become a classic, an important statement about man's relationship to the state. But it is also very much a product of its time. Published in 1849, it was written a year or so earlier, while Thoreau resided at Walden pond. This was a difficult period for the United States. The Missouri Compromise of 1820 had not settled the slavery issue, and northern radicals were becoming increasingly impatient with attempts to work out a political solution. The Mexican War, which broke out in 1846, had exacerbated this impatience, since it seemed to many like Thoreau an unjust war on a weaker state for the benefit of slaveholders. It is this background which gives Thoreau's essay its urgency. Like many other northern radicals, he was impatient of further compromise.

This looks like the introduction of an argumentative essay. It is not argumentative, however, because it does not set up a genuine problem. What the last sentence proposes is a pseudo-problem or pseudothesis. I have no intention of writing an essay about Thoreau's impatience. An introduction to a piece of reportorial writing very often sets up a question. But it had better be an innocuous question, because the writer has nothing available except innocuous answers.

At any rate I have an introduction, and I am ready to get into the body of my paper. Thoreau's opinion of the state seems the best place to begin; I will return to the points about the unimportance of government gathered under "B." I will need to begin with a topic sentence which my points can serve to support.

> This background accounts for Thoreau's attitude

From Argumentation to Reportorial Writing

toward government in general, which is very nearly an attitude of contempt. He begins his essay with a resounding assertion that "that government is best which governs least" and that the ideal is no government at all. While he thinks the American Constitution sets up as good a government as most [I just remembered that point], his contention is that no government accomplishes anything; only men make things happen. But government is not merely a pale neuter in human affairs; it is, finally, immoral. It represents the strength of the majority, and not justice, and its model citizen is the impassive soldier doing ceremonial guard duty—a spectacle which fills Thoreau with horror.

This paragraph is a very standard one in reportorial writing. The topic sentence is more general than topic sentences are apt to be in argumentation. Its function is really to enable me to bring forward my points as evidence supporting it. In organizing the points, I have merely moved from the more moderate to the more extreme. I am now ready to turn to the head marked "C," "The individual should act."

Obedience is not merely, for Thoreau, not a virtue; it is an enemy of virtue. [I have abstracted this transitional sentence from the point about the soldier.] For Thoreau, virtue is an active commitment to justice as that is determined by the conscience of the individual. He underscores the necessity for action upon one's opinions; the opinion which is not acted upon doesn't really count. Presumably the more positive the action is, the better, but he demands of the reader only a minimum course; the least one can do is not to support wrong. Since the payment of taxes is the point at which the citizen and his government most directly confront each other, it follows that nonpayment of taxes is the least the just man can do when confronted by an unjust government.

It is obvious that the issue for Thoreau is the obligation to act. He asserts that all agree that the citizen has the right to revolution in certain cases, and he thinks it is self-evident that the United States government in 1848 was more unjust than the British government had been in 1775. His problem is to get his fellow citizens to act upon these facts. Hence his insistence that the problem of slavery is not merely a southern problem, that Massachusetts is equally guilty for not doing anything about it. The essay is really directed at his fellow citizens who

From Argumentation to Reportorial Writing

want to wait for legal recourse against evil. A man doesn't have sufficient time in his life to exhaust constitutional means.

The whole problem in reportorial writing is the establishment of continuity. Perhaps half of each of these paragraphs is transitional material serving to join points.

It will be noticed that a problem developed in the writing; the points proved to be too disparate to be gathered easily into one paragraph. The obvious solution was to make two paragraphs out of them.

On an examination I would surely throw the remaining points, gathered under "A" and "C," into a kind of catchall conclusion. But since reportorial conclusions under ordinary circumstances are composed out of whole cloth and contain no information whatsoever, this demonstration paper will be more useful if we make a further paragraph out of these points. We can then invent a characteristic conclusion.

> At the same time, Thoreau is acutely aware of the obstacles to the kind of general action he wants. He knows that at best civil disobedience will be very much a minority movement. Public opinion will continue to be dominated by merchants more interested in money than morality. But in response to this fact he insists that even the smallest minority, even one man, can make all the difference. Furthermore, he knows the cost of civil disobedience to that minority. The point of the episode of his night in jail is that civil disobedience involves no personal cost. But, as he recognizes earlier, the participating individual must already have lost his stake in society—family and property.
>
> The significance of Thoreau's essay is hard to estimate. On the one hand, it presumes at least the existence of a noticeable minority utterly divorced from the ordinary concerns of society by its lack of property and the usual social ties. There is a question whether such a minority, so far divorced from the interests of the majority, could ever function as its conscience. On the other hand, there is no doubt that generations of Americans have been deeply moved by "On the Duty of Civil Disobedience." That this experience has not contributed to the American character is hard to imagine.

The first paragraph is organized in the way the ones previously analyzed were organized; it sets up a topic sentence broad enough to include the relevant points and attempts to keep these related. (The strain still remaining between the points under "A" and "D" is bridged by "furthermore.")

The last paragraph, the conclusion of the essay, perhaps sounds all right, but it says very little. "The significance of Thoreau's essay is hard to estimate" is hardly a resounding conclusion. But a reportorial conclusion with the force of an argumentative one would be severely out of place. This is apparent if one tries to imagine a specific and forthright conclusion to the above essay:

> "On the Duty of Civil Disobedience" is the beginning of a modern conception of the proper relationship between man and state. . . .
>
> Thoreau's conception of a split between society and government is unjustified. . . .
>
> The special circumstances of the 1850's make "On the Duty of Civil Disobedience" an eccentric statement of the citizen-state relationship. . . .

Any of these sentences can be imagined as an appropriate beginning sentence for the concluding paragraph of an argumentative essay. (They would of course be very different essays.) But they would not be appropriate for a reportorial essay. I have written an essay whose function was to convey information, not to establish a conclusion. A forthright statement in the last paragraph would probably be rejected by the reader; if it were not, it would mislead him.

The conclusion of a reportorial essay is in fact a pure structure. It can be seen as an esthetic necessity, the rounding-off of a piece of communication. It is more likely that the pseudo-argumentative structure leads the reader to expect a conclusion, even when what has gone before makes a genuine conclusion impossible. In any case, the student, like the professional writer, will do well to signal to his readers that the communication is at an end.

REPORTORIAL WRITING BY PSEUDOHISTORY

Reportorial writing by what might be called the historical method can be considered briefly. The procedure is much the same as for pseudoargumentation. The writer begins by gathering information and he organizes it into heads as well as he can. The writing problem is to relate these heads to each other by fair means or pseudomeans. When he can the writer organizes them chronologically, and when he cannot he will try to give the appearance of organizing them chronologically.[3]

Pseudohistory differs from pseudoargumentation in several ways. Pseudoargumentation must have an introduction; pseudohistory may or may not, just as a history book may or may not. (In most instances it will not.) A writer on the causes of the Civil War, for instance, may simply begin with the first event or cause he wishes to discuss: "The divisions in American opinion that ultimately led to the Civil War first became manifest after the Compromise of 1820." This sentence is not introductory; it is a topic sentence of a paragraph which will gather together a certain kind of information.

Second, pseudohistorical writing is much more likely to have inherent in its intention certain potential part-structures. It is particularly apt to have a series of points which have an obvious chronological relationship to each other. To begin with 1820 and end with 1865 is in some sense a "natural" proceeding, representing one kind of ordering. Any writer will make use of whatever structures he can lay hold of—before and after, front and behind, right and left. In reportorial writing, however, these will always be ways of organizing a part of the essay and not the whole of it. If the writer were able to use before-and-after as the organizing principle for his whole essay, he would in fact be writing history; the other structures would lead to guide books or recipes.

Third, the relationships among paragraphs or sections are usually managed differently. The writer's problem is that the break in continuity between the historical part-structures is ordinarily greater than the break between the paragraphs or sections of pseudoargumentation. Hence he requires more

[3] The basic difference between the pseudohistory of reportorial writing and history proper is to be found in the intentions of the respective writers. The historian is engaged in tracing a causal process; he is concerned with the series of events leading to such and such a consequence. The reportorial writer is engaged in giving information which does not, as a whole, have causal interrelationships. He will, of course, utilize the partial relationships that he has. A textbook in history, it should be pointed out, ordinarily makes use of both procedures.

From Argumentation to Reportorial Writing

transitional matter. But the next section will clarify this distinction.

We have discussed reportorial writing by the historical method as though it required a subject at least partly historical. This is not the case. Most current political writing as well as most foreign affairs studies, for instance, are written in this fashion. The major advantage of this method is probably in the *ethos* that it projects—that of the detached observer of the human scene.

PARAGRAPHING IN
REPORTORIAL WRITING

As was pointed out, the mark of reporting is that it must relate things which are not intrinsically related. In other words, the reporter must devise connections for paragraphs or part-structures consisting of several paragraphs which are in some sense artificial. The writer has essentially two methods at his disposal by which he can make such connections, the tailing paragraph and the attention-diverting transitional sentence. But to understand these connective devices it will be necessary to consider for a moment the standard paragraph structure of argumentation.

It was pointed out in Chapter 5 that the usual structure of an argumentative paragraph is a topic sentence followed by sentences which elaborate on that topic sentence or argue for it in some way. This supportive material in the paragraph, whether illustrative or demonstrative, will not be quite the same as the topic sentence; it will always move out in some direction from the proposition of that sentence. It is a common error in student writing to attempt to connect a paragraph with the last sentence of the previous paragraph; an argument can only get hopelessly lost when this kind of connection is made. An argumentative essay must move from topic sentence to topic sentence to maintain its direction.

But this is not the case in reportorial writing, which isn't going any place to begin with. Hence pseudoargumentation, particularly, can make very effective use of tailing paragraphs, paragraphs which are connected nose to tail like elephants in a circus. A single illustration will suffice.

From Argumentation to Reportorial Writing

The Missouri Compromise of 1820 is a good point from which to date the conflict which led to the Civil War. At the beginning of the nineteenth century the prevailing mood of the United States as a whole was nationalistic. The Louisiana Purchase, after some initial outcry, had caught the American imagination; the sense of a nation on the move, which was to be a powerful force after the Civil War, was already astir. Even the man who, above all others, was to be the spokesman for regionalism, John Calhoun, was a nationalist at this time.

John Calhoun is, in fact, a useful point of reference by which to trace the development of the conflict. . . .

This second paragraph, however it may go, does not make any essential connection with the topic sentence of the preceding paragraph. It is connected only to the last sentence of that paragraph, and that sentence is merely illustrative in the context of the paragraph. An argumentative essay which made such a connection would be damaged beyond redemption by it. But reportorial writing makes connections where it can. The tailed paragraphs have a sense of connection which will keep the reader reading, which is the point.

The second kind of connection upon which reportorial writing depends is the transitional sentence or short transitional paragraph. A transitional sentence is simply a kind of sign, inviting the reader to change the focus of his attention. An example would be:

The invention of the cotton gin by Eli Whitney in 1793 had profoundly influenced the Southern economy. Prior to that invention, the only profitable cotton crop was the long-fibered variety grown in the lowlands along the coast. The cotton gin made the short-fibered variety profitable, and this could be grown anywhere in the South. The result was that large plantations, dependent upon slave labor, very shortly came to dominate the economy of the entire region.

Meanwhile, however, the North was beginning to experience an economic revolution of its own. . . .

The transitional sentence which begins the second paragraph actually assures the reader that what follows is indeed relevant to what has gone before. There need not be as much

From Argumentation to Reportorial Writing

connection as there would presumably be in the foregoing example for the transitional sentence to function in this way.

In general, pseudoargumentation makes most use of the tailing paragraph, pseudohistory of transition. This observation is not, of course, a rule; the writer uses whatever will be useful in either kind of writing. In most instances the student does not need to worry about which transitional device he ought to use in a particular instance. He does not need to say to himself, "Ah, I need a tailing paragraph connection here," because he has encountered enough tailing paragraph connections and transitional sentences in his reading experience to have them available in his writing repertoire. The knowledge of these devices, like the knowledge of grammatical rules, functions remedially; it becomes applicable when the student recognizes that there is trouble someplace.

Conclusion

In reportorial writing as in argumentation, the most important procedures are the preliminary ones. The trick of such writing is the gathering of appropriate points into heads and the felicitous ordering of those heads. Thereafter the writer needs to be flexible. If the student has had sufficient experience in writing argumentation, his sense of movement will ordinarily be a reliable index of his success. Rapid writing is as advantageous in reportorial writing as it is in argumentation.

A word of caution is perhaps in order. When we say that a piece of reporting does not have a thesis, we do not mean that it has no point of view. The student writing an examination probably wants merely to demonstrate his fund of information. But the professional writer has a larger end in view. Reportorial writing is as persuasive in intention as argumentative writing. But its persuasive intent lies concealed in the selection of facts and in their ordering. Nor is there any way to escape this kind of subjectivity. The writer can only select from the enormous amount of information available on a particular subject, and he can only weigh his presentation of that information toward one point of view or another.

From Argumentation to Reportorial Writing

This point is easily demonstrated if the student will look again at the conclusion of the demonstration essay. As it reads, the paragraph is on the whole favorable to the notion that Thoreau has been an influential writer. But if we were simply to reverse the ordering of elements, putting the last sentence second in the paragraph, the judgment would be unfavorable. The point is that the paragraph must judge one way or the other simply because there is no way to say the two things simultaneously. The honest writer will say what he really thinks to be the case, but he cannot say what *is* the case.

EPILOGUE: THE STUDENT WRITER AND BEYOND

This book has had two limited objectives. First and most important, it has proposed procedures by means of which the student can introduce genuine movement into his writing. To repeat once more what has been said many times: the student who knows when his prose is moving and when it is not has crossed the chasm that separates the writer from the non-writer. In the second place, the student has learned to manage the structures and part-structures, the pseudostructures and transitions, with which the writer maintains his movement. Where does the student go from here?

The art of writing which is not available in a freshman writing course consists primarily of two things: (1) stylistic range and control, and (2) structural complexity.

The student's progress in these two skills depends much less upon his writing than upon his reading. The student who proposes to take writing seriously, beyond the final examination in the writing course, must become aware of style as an integral element in everything he reads. He must learn not merely to respond to effective style but to become aware of the kinds of diction and sentence and paragraph structure which give it its particular force. To become this sensitive to style, he must of course coordinate eye and ear. But the result of this kind of reading will become apparent in his own writing. Style no more than personality is fixed for all time. He will find, when he needs to write himself, that style comes increasingly within his power.

The complexity of professional essay-writing takes two forms. In the first place, professional writers do not often write 700-word essays, the usual limit for a student in a freshman writing course. But this does not mean that they do not write 700-word arguments over and over. The complexity of a long argumentative essay arises from the way arguments are combined in it. A writer frequently strings arguments together; the conclusion of one becomes the premise for another. Furthermore, he seldom confines himself to one argument. There may be a section in his essay refuting the opposing point of view and followed by two or three arguments which draw his own conclusion from different premises. Modern writers, particuarly, mix genres frequently—one finds that reportorial writing occurs in argumentative essays and vice versa. The student is probably capable of handling this kind of complexity any time he needs to; the actual writing presents no great difficulty if there is an occasion for the sustained mental effort of conceptualization.

The second kind of structural complexity that distinguishes professional writing from what the student has learned comes about through the systematic effort of some writers, especially modern ones, to conceal the bones of their enterprise, its structure. Skilled modern writers often paragraph in a peculiar way; they make paragraphs which are in fact logically connected look as though they are tailed; they conflate arguments—in short, they take great pains to make essays read as though they were continuous narratives. Again, these are skills which are learned and not taught. Such cunning is learned by long reading apprenticeship to masters.

The student who has mastered the writing techniques discussed in this book knows the basic crafts of writing. He is not by any means a master of the art, but he knows enough to become a master if he is willing, over some years, to put forth the effort.

ON THE DUTY OF CIVIL DISOBEDIENCE

Henry David Thoreau

I heartily accept the motto,—"That government is best which governs least;" and I should like to see it acted up to more rapidly and systematically. Carried out, it finally amounts to this, which also I believe,—"That government is best which governs not at all;" and when men are prepared for it, that will be the kind of government which they will have. Government is at best but an expedient; but most governments are usually, and all governments are sometimes, inexpedient. The objections which have been brought against a standing army, and they are many and weighty, and deserve to prevail, may also at last be brought against a standing government. The standing army is only an arm of the standing government. The government itself, which is only the mode which the people have chosen to execute their will, is equally liable to be abused and perverted before the people can act through it. Witness the present Mexican war, the work of comparatively a few individuals using the standing government as their tool; for, in the outset, the people would not have consented to this measure.

This American government,—what is it but a tradition, though a recent one, endeavoring to transmit itself unimpaired to posterity, but each instant losing some of its integrity? It has not the vitality and force of a single living man; for a single man can bend it to his will. It is a sort of wooden gun to the people themselves; and, if ever they should use it in earnest as a real one against each other, it will surely split. But it is not the less necessary for this; for the people must have some complicated machinery or other, and hear its din, to satisfy that idea of government which they have. Governments show thus how successfully men can be imposed on, even impose on themselves, for their own advantage. It is excellent, we must all allow; yet this government never of itself furthered any enterprise, but by the alacrity with which it got out of its way. *It* does not keep the country free. *It* does not settle the West. *It* does not educate. The character inherent in the American people has done all that has been accomplished; and it would have done somewhat more, if the government had not sometimes got in its way. For government is an expedient by which men would fain succeed in letting one another alone; and, as has been said, when it is most expedient, the governed are most let alone by it. Trade and commerce, if they were not made of India rubber, would never manage to bounce over the obstacles which legislators are continually putting in their way; and, if one were to judge these men wholly by the effects of their actions, and not partly by their intentions, they would deserve to be classed and punished with those mischievous persons who put obstructions on the railroads.

But, to speak practically and as a citizen, unlike those who call themselves no-government men, I ask for, not at once no government, but *at once* a better government. Let every man make known what kind of government would command his respect, and that will be one step toward obtaining it.

After all, the practical reason why, when the power is once in the hands of the people, a majority are permitted, and for a long period continue, to rule, is not because they are most likely to be in the right, nor because this seems fairest to the minority, but because they are physically the strongest. But a government in which the majority rule in all cases cannot be based on justice, even as far as men understand it. Can there not be a government in which majorities do not virtually decide right and wrong, but conscience?—in which majorities

On the Duty of Civil Disobedience

decide only those questions to which the rule of expediency is applicable? Must the citizen ever for a moment, or in the least degree, resign his conscience to the legislator? Why has every man a conscience, then? I think that we should be men first, and subjects afterward. It is not desirable to cultivate a respect for the law, so much as for the right. The only obligation which I have a right to assume, is to do at any time what I think right. It is truly enough said, that a corporation has no conscience; but a corporation of conscientious men is a corporation *with* a conscience. Law never made men a whit more just; and, by means of their respect for it, even the well-disposed are daily made the agents of injustice. A common and natural result of an undue respect for law is, that you may see a file of soldiers, colonel, captain, corporal, privates, powder-monkeys and all, marching in admirable order over hill and dale to the wars, against their wills, aye, against their common sense and consciences, which makes it very steep marching indeed, and produces a palpitation of the heart. They have no doubt that it is a damnable business in which they are concerned; they are all peaceably inclined. Now, what are they? Men at all? or small moveable forts and magazines, at the service of some unscrupulous man in power? Visit the Navy Yard, and behold a marine, such a man as an American government can make, or such as it can make a man with its black arts,—a mere shadow and reminisence of humanity, a man laid out alive and standing, and already, as one may say, buried under arms with funeral accompaniments, though it may be

> Not a drum was heard, nor a funeral note,
> As his corse to the ramparts we hurried;
> Not a soldier discharged his farewell shot
> O'er the grave where our hero we buried.

The mass of men serve the State thus, not as men mainly, but as machines, with their bodies. They are the standing army, and the militia, jailers, constables, *posse comitatus*, &c. In most cases there is no free exercise whatever of the judgment or of the moral sense; but they put themselves on a level with wood and earth and stones; and wooden men can perhaps be manufactured that will serve the purpose as well. Such command no more respect than men of straw, or a lump of dirt. They have the same sort of worth only as horses and dogs. Yet such as these even are commonly esteemed good citizens. Others, as most legislators, politicians, lawyers, ministers, and office-holders, serve the State chiefly with their heads; and, as they rarely make any moral distinctions, they are as likely to serve the devil, without *intending* it, as God. A very few, as heroes, patriots, martyrs, reformers in the great sense, and *men*, serve the State with their consciences also, and so necessarily resist it for the most part; and they are commonly treated by it as enemies. A wise man will only be useful as a man, and will not submit to be "clay," and "stop a hole to keep the wind away," but leave that office to his dust at least: —

> *I am too high-born to be propertied,*
> *To be a secondary at control,*
> *Or useful serving-man and instrument*
> *To any sovereign state throughout the world.*

He who gives himself entirely to his fellow-men appears to them useless and selfish; but he who gives himself partially to them is pronounced a benefactor and philanthropist.

How does it become a man to behave toward this American government to-day? I answer that he cannot without disgrace be associated with it. I cannot for an instant recognize that political organizations as *my* government which is the *slave's* government also.

All men recognize the right of revolution; that is, the right to refuse allegiance to and to resist the government, when its tyranny or its inefficiency are great and unendurable. But almost all say that such is not the case now. But such was the case, they think, in the Revolution of '75. If one were to tell me that this was a bad government because it taxed certain foreign commodities brought to its ports, it is most probable that I should not make an ado about it, for I can do without them: all machines have their friction, and possibly this does enough good to counterbalance the evil. At any rate, it is a great evil to make a stir about it. But when the friction comes to have its machine, and oppression and robbery are organized, I say, let us not have such a machine any longer. In other words, when a sixth of the population of a nation which has undertaken to be the refuge of liberty are slaves, and a whole country is unjustly overrun and conquered by a foreign army, and subjected to military law, I think that it is not too soon

On the Duty of Civil Disobedience

for honest men to rebel and revolutionize. What makes this duty the more urgent is the fact, that the country so overrun is not our own, but ours is the invading army.

Paley, a common authority with many on moral questions, in his chapter on the "Duty of Submission to Civil Government," resolves all civil obligation into expediency; and he proceeds to say, "that so long as the interest of the whole society requires it, that is, so long as the established government cannot be resisted or changed without public inconveniency, it is the will of God, that the established government be obeyed, and no longer."—"This principle being admitted, the justice of every particular case of resistance is reduced to a computation of the quantity of the danger and grievance on the one side, and of the probability and expense of redressing it on the other." Of this, he says, every man shall judge for himself. But Paley appears never to have contemplated those cases to which the rule of expediency does not apply, in which a people, as well as an individual, must do justice, cost what it may. If I have unjustly wrested a plank from a drowing man, I must restore it to him though I drown myself. This, according to Paley, would be inconvenient. But he that would save his life, in such a case, shall lose it. This people must cease to hold slaves, and to make war on Mexico, though it cost them their existence as a people.

In their practice, nations agree with Paley; but does any one think that Massachusetts does exactly what is right at the present crisis?

> A drab of state, a cloth-o'-silver slut,
> To have her train borne up, and her soul trail in the dirt.

Practically speaking, the opponents to a reform in Massachusetts are not a hundred thousand politicians at the South, but a hundred thousand merchants and farmers here, who are more interested in commerce and agriculture than they are in humanity, and are not prepared to do justice to the slave and to Mexico, *cost what it may.* I quarrel not with far-off foes, but with those who, near at home, co-operate with, and do the bidding of those far away, and without whom the latter would be harmless. We are accustomed to say, that the mass of men are unprepared; but improvement is slow, because the few are not materially wiser or better than the many. It is not so important that many should be as good as you, as that there be some absolute goodness somewhere; for that will leaven the whole lump. There are thousands who are *in opinion* opposed to slavery and to the war, who yet in effect do nothing to put an end to them; who, esteeming themselves children of Washington and Franklin, sit down with their hands in their pockets, and say that they know not what to do, and do nothing; who even postpone the question of freedom to the question of free-trade, and quietly read the prices-current along with the latest advices from Mexico, after dinner, and, it may be, fall asleep over them both. What is the price-current of an honest man and patriot to-day? They hesitate, and they regret, and sometimes they petition; but they do nothing in earnest and with effect. They will wait, well disposed, for others to remedy the evil, that they may no longer have it to regret. At most, they give only a cheap vote, and a feeble countenance and Godspeed, to the right, as it goes by them. There are nine hundred and ninety-nine patrons of virtue to one virtuous man; but it is easier to deal with the real possessor of a thing than with the temporary guardian of it.

All voting is a sort of gaming, like chequers or backgammon, with a slight moral tinge to it, a playing with right and wrong, with moral questions; and betting naturally accompanies it. The character of the voters is not staked. I cast my vote, perchance, as I think right; but I am not vitally concerned that that right should prevail. I am willing to leave it to the majority. Its obligation, therefore, never exceeds that of expediency. Even voting *for the right* is *doing* nothing for it. It is only expressing to men feebly your desire that it should prevail. A wise man will not leave the right to the mercy of chance, nor wish it to prevail through the power of the majority. There is but little virtue in the action of masses of men. When the majority shall at length vote for the abolition of slavery, it will be because they are indifferent to slavery, or because there is but little slavery left to be abolished by their vote. *They* will then be the only slaves. Only *his* vote can hasten the abolition of slavery who asserts his own freedom by his vote.

I hear of a convention to be held at Baltimore, or elsewhere, for the selection of a candidate for the Presidency, made up chiefly of editors, and men who are politicians by profession; but I think, what is it to any independent, intelligent, and respectable man what decision they may come to, shall we not have the advantage of his wisdom and honesty, nevertheless? Can we not count upon some independent votes? Are there

On the Duty of Civil Disobedience

not many individuals in the country who do not attend conventions? But no: I find that the respectable man, so called, has immediately drifted from his position, and despairs of his country, when his country has more reason to despair of him. He forthwith adopts one of the candidates thus selected as the only *available* one, thus proving that he is himself *available* for any purposes of the demagogue. His vote is of no more worth than that of any unprincipled foreigner or hireling native, who may have been bought. Oh for a man who is a *man*, and, as my neighbor says, has a bone in his back which you cannot pass your hand through! Our statistics are at fault: the population has been returned too large. How many *men* are there to a square thousand miles in this country? Hardly one. Does not America offer any inducement for men to settle here? The American has dwindled into an Odd Fellow,— one who may be known by the development of his organ of gregariousness, and a manifest lack of intellect and cheerful self-reliance; whose first and chief concern, on coming into the world, is to see that the alms-houses are in good repair; and, before yet he has lawfully donned the virile garb, to collect a fund for the support of the widows and orphans that may be; who, in short, ventures to live only by the aid of the mutual insurance company, which has promised to bury him decently.

It is not a man's duty, as a matter of course, to devote himself to the eradication of any, even the most enormous wrong; he may still properly have other concerns to engage him; but it is his duty, at least, to wash his hands of it, and, if he gives it no thought longer, not to give it practically his support. If I devote myself to other pursuits and contemplations, I must first see, at least, that I do not pursue them sitting upon another man's shoulders. I must get off him first, that he may pursue his contemplations too. See what gross inconsistency is tolerated. I have heard some of my townsmen say, "I should like to have them order me out to help put down an insurrection of the slaves, or to march to Mexico,—see if I would go;" and yet these very men have each, directly by their allegiance, and so indirectly, at least, by their money, furnished a substitute. The soldier is applauded who refuses to serve in an unjust war by those who do not refuse to sustain the unjust government which makes the war; is applauded by those whose own act and authority he disregards and sets at nought; as if the State were penitent to that degree that it hired one to scourge it while it sinned, but not to that degree that it left off sinning for a moment. Thus, under the name of order and civil government, we are all made at last to pay homage to and support our own meanness. After the first blush of sin, comes its indifference; and from immoral it becomes, as it were, *un*moral, and not quite unnecessary to that life which we have made.

The broadest and most prevalent error requires the most disinterested virtue to sustain it. The slight reproach to which the virtue of patriotism is commonly liable, the noble are most likely to incur. Those who, while they disapprove of the character and measures of a government, yield to it their allegiance and support, are undoubtedly its most conscientious supporters, and so frequently the most serious obstacles to reform. Some are petitioning the State to dissolve the Union, to disregard the requisitions of the President. Why do they not dissolve it themselves,—the union between themselves and the State,—and refuse to pay their quota into its treasury? Do not they stand in the same relation to this State, that the State does to the Union? And have not the same reasons prevented the State from resisting the Union, which have prevented them from resisting the State?

How can a man be satisfied to entertain an opinion merely, and enjoy *it?* Is there any enjoyment in it, if his opinion is that he is aggrieved? If you are cheated out of a single dollar by your neighbor, you do not rest satisfied with knowing that you are cheated, or with saying that you are cheated, or even with petitioning him to pay you your due; but you take effectual steps at once to obtain the full amount, and see that you are never cheated again. Action from principle,—the perception and the performance of right,—changes things and relations; it is essentially revolutionary, and does not consist wholly with any thing which was. It not only divides states and churches, it divides families, aye, it divides the *individual,* separating the diabolical in him from the divine.

Unjust laws exist; shall we be content to obey them, or shall we endeavor to amend them, and obey them until we have succeeded, or shall we transgress them at once? Men generally, under such a government as this, think that they ought to wait until they have persuaded the majority to alter them. They think that, if they should resist, the remedy would be worse than the evil. But it is the fault of the government itself that the remedy *is* worse than the evil. *It* makes it worse. Why is

On the Duty of Civil Disobedience

it not more apt to anticipate and provide for reform? Why does it not cherish its wise minority? Why does it cry and resist before it is hurt? Why does it not encourage its citizens to be on the alert to point out its faults, and *do* better than it would have them? Why does it always crucify Christ, and excommunicate Copernicus and Luther, and pronounce Washington and Franklin rebels?

One would think, that a deliberate and practical denial of its authority, was the only offense never contemplated by government; else, why has it not assigned its definite, its suitable and proportionate penalty? If a man who has no property refuses but once to earn nine shillings for the State, he is put in prison for a period unlimited by any law that I know, and determined only by the discretion of those who placed him there; but if he should steal ninety times nine shillings from the State, he is soon permitted to go at large again.

If the injustice is part of the necessary friction of the machine of government, let it go, let it go; perchance it will wear smooth,—certainly the machine will wear out. If the injustice has a spring, or a pulley, or a rope, or a crank, exclusively for itself, then perhaps you may consider whether the remedy will not be worse than the evil; but if it is of such a nature that it requires you to be the agent of injustice to another, then, I say, break the law. Let your life be a counter friction to stop the machine. What I have to do is to see, at any rate, that I do not lend myself to the wrong which I condemn.

As for adopting the ways which the State has provided for remedying the evil, I know not of such ways. They take too much time, and a man's life will be gone. I have other affairs to attend to. I came into this world, not chiefly to make this a good place to live in, but to live in it, be it good or bad. A man has not every thing to do, but something; and because he cannot do *every thing*, it is not necessary that he should do *something* wrong. It is not my business to be petitioning the governor or the legislature any more than it is theirs to petition me; and, if they should not hear my petition, what should I do then? But in this case the State has provided no way: its very Constitution is the evil. This may seem to be harsh and stubborn and unconciliatory; but it is to treat with the utmost kindness and consideration the only spirit that can appreciate or deserve it. So is all change for the better, like birth and death which convulse the body.

I do not hesitate to say, that those who call themselves abolitionists should at once effectually withdraw their support, both in person and property, from the government of Massachusetts, and not wait till they constitute a majority of one, before they suffer the right to prevail through them. I think that it is enough if they have God on their side, without waiting for that other one. Moreover, any man more right than his neighbors, constitutes a majority of one already.

I meet this American government, or its representative the State government, directly, and face to face, once a year, no more, in the person of its tax-gatherer; this is the only mode in which a man situated as I am necessarily meets it; and it then says distinctly, Recognize me; and the simplest, the most effectual, and, in the present pasture of affairs, the indispensablest mode of treating with it on this head, of expressing your little satisfaction with and love for it, is to deny it then. My civil neighbor, the tax-gatherer, is the very man I have to deal with,—for it is, after all, with men and not with parchment that I quarrel,—and he has voluntarily chosen to be an agent of the government. How shall he ever know well what he is and does as an officer of the government, or as a man, until he is obliged to consider whether he shall treat me, his neighbor, for whom he has respect, as a neighbor and well-disposed man, or as a maniac and disturber of the peace, and see if he can get over this obstruction to his neighborliness without a ruder and more impetuous thought or speech corresponding with his action? I know this well, that if one thousand, if one hundred, if ten men whom I could name,—if ten *honest* men only,—aye, if *one* HONEST man, in this State of Massachusetts, *ceasing to hold slaves,* were actually to withdraw from this copartnership, and be locked up in the county jail therefor, it would be the abolition of slavery in America. For it matters not how small the beginning may seem to be: what is once well done is done for ever. But we love better to talk about it: that we say is our mission. Reform keeps many scores of newspapers in its service, but not one man. If my esteemed neighbor, the State's ambassador, who will devote his days to the settlement of the question of human rights in the Council Chamber, instead of being threatened with the prisons of Carolina, were to sit down the prisoner of Massachusetts, that State which is so anxious to foist the sin of slavery upon her sister,—though at present she can discover only an act of inhospitality to be the ground of a quarrel with her,—the Legislature would not wholly waive the subject the following winter.

Under a government which imprisons any unjustly, the true place for a just man is also a prison. The proper place to-day, the only place which Massachusetts has provided for her freer and less desponding spirits, is in her prisons, to be put out and locked out of the State by her own act, as they have already put themselves out by their principles. It is there that the fugitive slave, and the Mexican prisoner on parole, and the Indian come to plead the wrongs of his race, should find them; on that separate, but more free and honorable ground, where the State places those who are not *with* her but *against* her,— the only house in a slave-state in which a free man can abide with honor. If any think that their influence would be lost there, and their voices no longer afflict the ear of the State, that they would not be as an enemy within its walls, they do not know by how much truth is stronger than error, nor how much more eloquently and effectively he can combat injustice who has experienced a little in his own person. Cast your whole vote, not a strip of paper merely, but your whole influence. A minority is powerless while it conforms to the majority; it is not even a minority then; but it is irresistible when it clogs by its whole weight. If the alternative is to keep all just men in prison, or give up war and slavery, the State will not hesitate which to choose. If a thousand men were not to pay their tax-bills this year, that would not be a violent and bloody measure, as it would be to pay them, and enable the State to commit violence and shed innocent blood. This is, in fact, the definition of a peaceable revolution, if any such is possible. If the tax-gatherer, or any other public officer, asks me, as one has done, "But what shall I do?" my answer is, "If you really wish to do any thing, resign your office." When the subject has refused allegiance, and the officer has resigned his office, then the revolution is accomplished. But even suppose blood should flow. Is there not a sort of blood shed when the conscience is wounded? Through this wound a man's real manhood and immortality flow out, and he bleeds to an everlasting death. I see this blood flowing now.

I have contemplated the imprisonment of the offender, rather than the seizure of his goods,—though both will serve the same purpose,—because they who assert the purest right, and consequently are most dangerous to a corrupt State, commonly have not spent much time in accumulating property. To such the State renders comparatively small services, and a slight tax is wont to appear exorbitant, particularly if they are obliged to earn it by special labor with their hands. If they were one who lived wholly without the use of money, the State itself would hesitate to demand it of him. But the rich man—not to make any invidious comparison—is always sold to the institution which makes him rich. Absolutely speaking, the more money, the less virtue; for money comes between a man and his objects, and obtains them for him; and it was certainly no great virtue to obtain it. It puts to rest many questions which he would otherwise be taxed to answer; while the only new question which it puts is the hard but superfluous one, how to spend it. Thus his moral ground is taken from under his feet. The opportunities of living are diminished in proportion as what are called the "means" are increased. The best thing a man can do for his culture when he is rich is to endeavor to carry out those schemes which he entertained when he was poor. Christ answered the Herodians according to their condition. "Show me the tribute-money," said he;—and one took a penny out of his pocket;—If you use money which has the image of Caesar on it, and which he has made current and valuable, that is, *if you are men of the State,* and gladly enjoy the advantages of Caesar's government, then pay him back some of his own when he demands it; "Render therefore to Caesar that which is Caesar's, and to God those things which are God's,"—leaving them no wiser than before as to which was which; for they did not wish to know.

When I converse with the freest of my neighbors, I perceive that, whatever they may say about the magnitude and seriousness of the question, and their regard for the public tranquility, the long and the short of the matter is, that they cannot spare the protection of the existing government, and they dread the consequences of disobedience to it to their property and families. For my own part, I should not like to think that I ever rely on the protection of the State. But, if I deny the authority of the State when it presents its tax-bill, it will soon take and waste all my property, and so harass me and my children without end. This is hard. This makes it impossible for a man to live honestly and at the same time comfortably in outward respects. It will not be worth the while to accumulate property; that would be sure to go again. You must hire or squat somewhere, and raise but a small crop, and

On the Duty of Civil Disobedience

eat that soon. You must live within yourself, and depend upon yourself, always tucked up and ready for a start, and not have many affairs. A man may grow rich in Turkey even, if he will be in all respects a good subject of the Turkish government. Confucius said,—"If a State is governed by the principles of reason, poverty and misery are subjects of shame; if a State is not governed by the principles of reason, riches and honors are the subjects of shame." No: until I want the protection of Massachusetts to be extended to me in some distant southern port, where my liberty is endangered, or until I am bent solely on building up an estate at home by peaceful enterprise, I can afford to refuse allegiance to Massachusetts, and her right to my property and life. It costs me less in every sense to incur the penalty of disobedience to the State, than it would to obey. I should feel as if I were worth less in that case.

Some years ago, the State met me in behalf of the church, and commanded me to pay a certain sum toward the support of a clergyman whose preaching my father attended, but never I myself. "Pay," it said, "or be locked up in the jail." I declined to pay. But, unfortunately another man saw fit to pay it. I did not see why the schoolmaster should be taxed to support the priest, and not the priest the schoolmaster: for I was not the State's schoolmaster, but I supported myself by voluntary subscription. I did not see why the lyceum should not present its tax-bill, and have the State to back its demand, as well as the church. However, at the request of the select-men, I condescended to make some such statement as this in writing:—"Know all men by these presents, that I, Henry Thoreau, do not wish to be regarded as a member of any in-corporated society which I have not joined." This I gave to the town-clerk; and he has it. The State, having thus learned that I did not wish to be regarded as a member of that church, has never made a like demand on me since; though it said that it must adhere to its original presumption that time. If I had known how to name them, I should then have signed off in detail from all the societies which I never signed on to; but I did not know where to find a complete list.

I have paid no poll-tax for six years. I was put into a jail once on this account, for one night; and, as I stood considering the walls of solid stone, two or three feet thick, the door of wood and iron, a foot thick, and the iron grating which strained the light, I could not help being struck with the foolishness of that institution which treated me as if I were mere flesh and blood and bones, to be locked up. I wondered that it should have concluded at length that this was the best use it could put me to, and had never thought to avail itself of my services in some way. I saw that, if there was a wall of stone between me and my townsmen, there was a still more difficult one to climb or break through, before they could get to be as free as I was. I did not for a moment feel confined, and the walls seemed a great waste of stone and mortar. I felt as if I alone of all my townsmen had paid my tax. They plainly did not know how to treat me, but behaved like persons who are underbred. In every threat and in every compliment there was a blunder; for they thought that my chief desire was to stand the other side of that stone wall. I could not but smile to see how industriously they locked the door on my meditations, which followed them out again without let or hindrance, and *they* were really all that was dangerous. As they could not reach me, they had resolved to punish my body; just as boys, if they cannot came at some person aganst whom they have a spite, will abuse his dog. I saw that the State was half-witted, that it was timid as a lone woman with her silver spoons, and that it did not know its friends from its foes, and I lost all my remaining respect for it, and pitied it.

Thus the State never intentionally confronts a man's sense, intellectual or moral, but only his body, his senses. It is not armed with superior wit or honesty, but with superior physical strength. I was not born to be forced. I will breathe after my own fashion. Let us see who is the strongest. What force has a multitude? They only can force me who obey a higher law than I. They force me to become like themselves. I do not hear of *men* being *forced* to live this way or that by masses of men. What sort of life were that to live? When I meet a government which says to me, "Your money or your life," why should I be in haste to give it my money? It may be in a great strait, and not know what to do: I cannot help that. It must help itself: do as I do. It is not worth the while to snivel about it. I am not responsible for the successful working of the machinery of society. I am not the son of the engineer. I perceive that, when an acorn and a chestnut fall side by side, the one does not remain inert to make way for the other, but both obey their own laws, and spring and grow and flourish as best they can, till one, perchance, overshadows and destroys the other. If a

On the Duty of Civil Disobedience

plant cannot live according to its nature, it dies; and so a man.

The night in prison was novel and interesting enough. The prisoners in their shirt-slevees were enjoying a chat and the evening air in the doorway, when I entered. But the jailer said, "Come, boys, it is time to lock up," and so they dispersed, and I heard the sound of their steps returning into the hollow apartments. My roommate was introduced to me by the jailer, as "a first-rate fellow and a clever man." When the door was locked, he showed me where to hang my hat, and how he managed matters there. The rooms were whitewashed once a month; and this one, at least, was the whitest, most simply furnished, and probably the neatest apartment in the town. He naturally wanted to know where I came from, and what brought me there; and, when I had told him, I asked him in my turn how he came there, presuming him to be an honest man, of course; and, as the world goes, I believe he was. "Why," said he, "they accuse me of burning a barn; but I never did it." As near as I could discover, he had probably gone to bed in a barn when drunk, and smoked his pipe there; and so a barn was burnt. He had the reputation of being a clever man, had been there some three months waiting for his trial to come on, and would have to wait as much longer; but he was quite domesticated and contented, since he got his board for nothing, and thought that he was well treated.

He occupied one window, and I the other; and I saw, that, if one stayed there long, his principal business would be to look out the window. I had soon read all the tracts that were left there, and examined where former prisoners had broken out, and where a grate had been sawed off, and heard the history of the various occupants of that room; for I found that even here there was a history and a gossip which never circulated beyond the walls of the jail. Probably this is the only house in the town where verses are composed, which are afterward printed in circular form, but not published. I was shown quite a long list of verses which were composed by some young men who had been detected in an attempt to escape, who avenged themselves by singing them.

I pumped my fellow-prisoner as dry as I could, for fear I should never see him again; but at length he showed me which was my bed, and left me to blow out the lamp.

It was like travelling into a far country, such as I had never expected to behold, to lie there for one night. It seemed to me that I never had heard the town-clock strike before, nor the evening sounds of the village; for we slept with the windows open, which were inside the grating. It was to see my native village in the light of the middle ages, and our Concord was turned into a Rhine stream, and visions of knights and castles passed before me. They were the voices of old burghers that I heard in the streets. I was an involuntary spectator and auditor of whatever was done and said in the kitchen of the adjacent village-inn,—a wholly new and rare experience to me. It was a closer view of my native town. I was fairly inside of it. I never had seen its institutions before. This is one of its peculiar institutions; for it is a shire town. I began to comprehend what its inhabitants were about.

In the morning, our breakfasts were put through the hole in the door, in small oblong-square tin pans, made to fit, and holding a pint of chocolate, with brown bread, and an iron spoon. When they called for the vessels again, I was green enough to return what bread I had left, but my comrade seized it, and said that I should lay that up for lunch or dinner. Soon after, he was let out to work at haying in a neighboring field, whither he went every day, and would not be back till noon; so he bade me good-day, saying that he doubted if he should see me again.

When I came out of prison,—for some one interfered, and paid that tax,—I did not perceive that great changes had taken place on the common, such as he observed who went in a youth, and emerged a tottering and gray-headed man; and yet a change had to my eyes come over the scene,—the town, and State and country,—greater than any that mere time could effect. I saw yet more distinctly the State in which I lived. I saw to what extent the people among whom I lived could be trusted as good neighbors and friends; that their friendship was for summer weather only; that they did not greatly propose to do right; that they were a distinct race from me by their prejudices and superstitions, as the Chinamen and Malays are; that, in their sacrifices to humanity, they ran no risks, not even to their property; that, after all, they were not so noble but they treated the thief as he had treated them, and hoped, by a certain outward observance and a few prayers, and by walking in a particular straight though useless path from time to time, to save their souls. This may be to judge my

On the Duty of Civil Disobedience

117

neighbors harshly; for I believe that many of them are not aware that they have such an institution as the jail in their village.

It was formerly the custom in our village, when a poor debtor came out of jail, for his acquaintances to salute him, looking through their fingers, which were crossed to represent the grating of a jail window, "How do ye do?" My neighbors did not thus salute me, but first looked at me, and then at one another, as if I had returned from a long journey. I was put into jail as I was going to the shoemaker's to get a shoe which was mended. When I was let out the next morning, I proceeded to finish my errand, and, having put on my mended shoe, joined a huckleberry party, who were impatient to put themselves under my conduct; and in half an hour,—for the horse was soon tackled,—was in the midst of a huckleberry field, on one of our highest hills, two miles off, and then the State was nowhere to be seen.

This is the whole history of "My Prisons."

I have never declined paying the highway tax, because I am as desirous of being a good neighbor as I am of being a bad subject; and, as for supporting schools, I am doing my part to educate my fellow-countrymen now. It is for no particular item in the tax-bill that I refuse to pay it. I simply wish to refuse allegiance to the State, to withdraw and stand aloof from it effectually. I do not care to trace the course of my dollar, if I could, till it buys a man, or a musket to shoot one with, —the dollar is innocent,—but I am concerned to trace the effects of my allegiance. In fact, I quietly declare war with the State, after my fashion, though I will still make what use and get what advantage of her I can, as is usual in such cases.

If others pay the tax which is demanded of me, from a sympathy with the State, they do but what they have already done in their own case, or rather they abet injustice to a greater extent than the State requires. If they pay the tax from a mistaken interest in the individual taxed, to save his property, or prevent his going to jail, it is because they have not considered wisely how far they let their private feelings interfere with the public good.

This, then, is my position at present. But one cannot be too much on his guard in such a case, lest his action be biased by obstinacy, or an undue regard for the opinions of men. Let him see that he does only what belongs to himself and to the hour.

I think sometimes, Why, this people mean well; they are only ignorant; they would do better if they knew how; why give your neighbors this plain to treat you as they are not inclined to? But I think, again, This is no reason why I should do as they do, or permit others to suffer much greater pain of a different kind. Again, I sometimes say to myself, When many millions of men, without heat, without ill-will, without personal feeling of any kind, demand of you a few shillings only, without the possibility, such is their constitution, of retracting or altering their present demand, and without the possibility, on your side, of appeal to any other millions, why expose yourself to this overwhelming brute force? You do not resist cold and hunger, the winds and the waves, thus obstinately; you quietly submit to a thousand similar necessities. You do not put your head into the fire. But just in proportion as I regard this as not wholly a brute force, but partly a human force, and consider that I have relations to those millions as to so many millions of men, and not of mere brute or inanimate things, I see that appeal is possible, first and instantaneously, from them to the Maker of them, and, secondly, from them to themselves. But, if I put my head deliberately into the fire, there is no appeal to fire or to the Maker of fire, and I have only myself to blame. If I could convince myself that I have any right to be satisfied with men as they are, and to treat them accordingly, and not according, in some respects, to my requisitions and expectations of what they and I ought to be, then, like a good Mussulman and fatalist, I should endeavor to be satisfied with things as they are, and say it is the will of God. And, above all, there is this difference between resisting this and a purely brute or natural force, that I can resist this with some effect; but I cannot expect, like Orpheus, to change the nature of the rocks and trees and beasts.

I do not wish to quarrel with any man or nation. I do not wish to split hairs, to make fine distinctions, or set myself up as better than my neighbors. I seek rather, I may say, even an excuse for conforming to the laws of the land. I am but too ready to conform to them. Indeed, I have reason to suspect myself on this head; and each year, as the tax-gatherer comes round, I find myself disposed to review the acts and position of the general and State governments, and the spirit of the people, to discover a pretext for conformity.

On the Duty of Civil Disobedience

> We must affect our country as our parents,
> And if at any time we alienate
> Our love or industry from doing it honor,
> We must respect affects and teach the soul
> Matter of conscience and religion,
> And not desire of rule or benefit.

I believe that the State will soon be able to take all my work of this sort out of my hands, and then I shall be no better a patriot than my fellow-country-men. Seen from a lower point of view, the Constitution, with all its faults, is very good; the law and the courts are very respectable; even this State and this American government are, in many respects, very admirable and rare things, to be thankful for, such as a great many have described them; but seen from a point of view a little higher, they are what I have described them; seen from a higher still, and the highest, who shall say what they are, or that they are worth looking at or thinking of at all?

However, the government does not concern me much, and I shall bestow the fewest possible thoughts on it. It is not many moments that I live under a government, even in this world. If a man is thought-free, fancy-free, imagination-free, that which is *not* never for a long time appearing *to be* to him, unwise rulers or reformers cannot fatally interrupt him.

I know that most men think differently from myself; but those whose lives are by profession devoted to the study of these or kindred subjects, content me as little as any. States-men and legislators, standing so completely within the institution, never distinctly and nakedly behold it. They speak of moving society, but have no resting-place without it. They may be men of a certain experience and discrimination, and have no doubt invented ingenious and even useful systems, for which we sincerely thank them; but all their wit and use-fulness lie within certain not very wide limits. They are wont to forget that the world is not governed by policy and expe-diency. Webster never goes behind government, and so cannot speak with authority about it. His words are wisdom to those legislators who contemplate no essential reform in the existing government; but for thinkers, and those who legislate for all time, he never once glances at the subject. I know of those whose serene and wise speculations on this theme would soon reveal the limits of his mind's range and hospitality. Yet, com-pared with the cheap professions of most reformers, and the still cheaper wisdom and eloquence of politicians in general, his are almost the only sensible and valuable words, and we thank Heaven for him. Comparatively, he is always strong, original, and, above all, practical. Still his quality is not wisdom, but prudence. The lawyer's truth is not truth, but consistency, or a consistent expediency. Truth is always in harmony with herself, and is not concerned chiefly to reveal the justice that may consist with wrong-doing. He well deserves to be called, as he has been called, the Defender of the Constitution. There are really no blows to be given by him but defensive ones. He is not a leader, but a follower. His leaders are the men of '87. "I have never made an effort," he says, "and never propose to make an effort; I have never countenanced an effort, and never mean to countenance an effort, to disturb the arrangement as originally made, by which the various States came into the Union." Still thinking of the sanction which the Constitution gives to slavery, he says, "Because it was a part of the original compact,—let it stand." Notwithstanding his special acuteness and ability, he is unable to take a fact out of its merely political relations, and behold it as it lies absolutely to be disposed of by the intellect,— what, for instance, it behooves a man to do here in America to-day with regard to slavery, but ventures, or is driven, to make some such desperate answer as the following, while professing to speak absolutely, and as a private man,—from which what new and singular code of social duties might be inferred?—"The manner," says he, "in which the governments of those States where slavery exists are to regulate it, is for their own consideration, under their responsibility to their constituents, to the general laws of propriety, humanity, and justice, and to God. Associations formed elsewhere springing from a feeling of humanity, or any other cause, have nothing whatever to do with it. They have never received any encouragement from me, and they never will."[1]

They who know of no purer sources of truth, who have traced up its stream no higher, stand, and wisely stand, by the Bible and the Constitution, and drink at it there with reverence and humility; but they who behold where it comes trickling into this lake or that pool, gird up their loins once more, and continue their pilgrimage toward its fountain-head.

[1] These extracts have been inserted since the lecture was read.

On the Duty of Civil Disobedience

No man with a genius for legislation has appeared in America. They are rare in the history of the world. There are orators, politicians, and eloquent men, by the thousand; but the speaker has not yet opened his mouth to speak, who is capable of settling the much-vexed questions of the day. We love eloquence for its own sake, and not for any truth which it may utter, or any heroism it may inspire. Our legislators have not yet learned the comparative value of free-trade and of freedom, of union, and of rectitude, to a nation. They have no genius or talent for comparatively humble questions of taxation and finance, commerce and manufacturers and agriculture. If we were left solely to the wordy wit of legislators in Congress for our guidance, uncorrected by the seasonable experience and the effectual complaints of the people, America would not long retain her rank among the nations. For eighteen hundred years, though perchance I have no right to say it, the New Testament has been written; yet where is the legislator who has wisdom and practical talent enough to avail himself of the light which it sheds on the science of legislation?

The authority of government, even such as I am willing to submit to,—for I will cheerfully obey those who know and can do better than I, and in many things even those who neither know nor can do so well,—is still an impure one: to be strictly just, it must have the sanction and consent of the governed. It can have no pure right over my person and property but what I concede to it. The progress from an absolute to a limited monarchy, from a limited monarchy to a democracy, is a progress toward a true respect for the individual. Even the Chinese philosopher was wise enough to regard the individual as the basis of the empire. Is a democracy, such as we know it, the last improvement possible in government? Is it not possible to take a step further towards recognizing and organizing the rights of man? There will never be a really free and enlightened State, until the State comes to recognize the individual as a higher and independent power, from which all its own power and authority are derived, and treats him accordingly. I please myself with imagining a State at last which can afford to be just to all men, and to treat the individual with respect as a neighbor; which even would not think it inconsistent with its own repose, if a few were to live aloof from it, not meddling with it, nor embraced by it, who fulfilled all the duties of neighbors and fellow-men. A State which bore this kind of fruit, and suffered it to drop off as fast

On the Duty of Civil Disobedience

as it ripened, would prepare the way for a still more perfect and glorious State, which also I have imagined, but not yet anywhere seen.